REACHING OUTWARD AND UPWARD
···

IAN MacPHERSON

REACHING OUTWARD AND UPWARD
THE UNIVERSITY OF VICTORIA, 1963–2013

Published for THE UNIVERSITY OF VICTORIA by
McGILL-QUEEN'S UNIVERSITY PRESS | MONTREAL & KINGSTON | LONDON | ITHACA

© McGill-Queen's University Press 2012
ISBN 978-0-7735-4032-3

Legal deposit third quarter 2012
Bibliothèque nationale du Québec

Printed in Canada on acid-free paper.

McGill-Queen's University Press acknowledges the support of the
Canada Council for the Arts for our publishing program. We also
acknowledge the financial support of the Government of Canada
through the Canada Book Fund for our publishing activities.

Library and Archives Canada Cataloguing in Publication

MacPherson, Ian, 1939–
Reaching outward and upward : the University of Victoria,
1963–2013 / Ian MacPherson.

Includes bibliographical references and index.
ISBN 978-0-7735-4032-3

1. University of Victoria (B.C.) – History.   2. University of Victoria
(B.C.) – Presidents – History. 3. University cooperation – British
Columbia – Victoria – History.   I. Title.

LE3.B88M33 2012   378.711'28   C2012-901057-X

Set in 10.3/14 Warnock Pro with Avenir
Book design & typesetting by Garet Markvoort, zijn digital

··· THE SEASONS AT UVIC ···

CONTENTS

PRESIDENT'S PREFACE

As the University of Victoria prepares to celebrate its fiftieth anniversary, we can all take pride in its tradition of excellence. Established in 1963, building on the dual tradition of Victoria College and the Provincial Normal School, UVic has developed into one of Canada's – and indeed the world's – best universities.

To help us understand UVic's trajectory over the past five decades, Dr Ian MacPherson has written *Reaching Outward and Upward: The University of Victoria, 1963–2013*. Dr MacPherson is professor emeritus in our Department of History, former dean of the Faculty of Humanities, and founding director of the Centre for Co-operative and Community-Based Economy. He is an eminent historian and an exemplary UVic citizen, committed to university life, to scholarship, and to cooperation with the broader community.

In this instructive and beautiful volume, Ian MacPherson provides us with an overview of the different historical phases in the growth and development of our university, together with insights, recollections, and reflections. On behalf of all our colleagues at the University of Victoria, I would like to express our deepest gratitude for this major contribution to our anniversary.

David H. Turpin, CM, PhD, FRSC
University of Victoria President and Vice-Chancellor
Victoria
March 2012

FOREWORD AND ACKNOWLEDGMENTS

It has been an honour and a pleasure to work with others in developing this book celebrating the fiftieth anniversary of the University of Victoria (UVic). The book acknowledges, with respect and appreciation, the remarkable contribution made by its predecessor institution, Victoria College, from 1903 to 1963. It emphasizes the roles that communities – on and off campus – have played and are playing. It explores some of the many ways of knowing associated with UVic over the last fifty years.

It is an historical essay, not a history, as historians usually think about their work. It does not pretend to tell the "full story" of the university. It examines several issues only partly and ignores some because of space limitations. It passes over too quickly or even ignores the contributions of many outstanding people associated with UVic because of space concerns, a limitation I greatly regret. I hope they will understand. Another writer will hopefully fill in these gaps some years hence.

This book is based partly on archival research, but mostly it reflects insights gathered from interviews with some 160 people, all with strong associations with UVic. It relies heavily on examples for "proof," not the most conclusive form of evidence perhaps, but the one that best fits the book.

There are many people to thank. First and foremost, I am grateful to Elizabeth MacPherson for her understanding while the book was being prepared.

The list of other people to whom I am indebted is long. They include:

- President David Turpin for giving me the opportunity to prepare it and to write it as I wished;
- Vice-President Valerie Kuehne, Administrative Manager Shirley Lyon, and their colleagues in the External Relations office for their direction and support;
- UVic Communications, associated with the same office, particularly its director, Bruce Kilpatrick, and Robie Liscomb; Nick Clewley and Christina Marshall of the Marketing Department; and Anne Pattison, for their help in putting the book together, especially the visual dimensions of it;
- The members of the advisory committee that helped me avoid many errors (but are in no way responsible for the ones that remain): Eve

Chapple, graduate student; Ludgard De Decker, director, Office of the President; Nels Granewall, Student Awards and Financial Aid Services (retired); Ed Ishiguro, Biochemistry and Microbiology; Bruce Kilpatrick, director, Communications; Peter Liddell, professor emeritus, Germanic and Russian Studies; Morag MacNeil, University Secretary's Office; John McLaren, professor emeritus, Faculty of Law; Mary Sanseverino, acting associate director, Learning and Teaching Centre, and senior instructor, Computer Science; Christine St Peter, professor emerita, Women's Studies; and Martin Taylor, president and CEO, Ocean Networks Canada, Geography. I particularly wish to thank Mary Sanseverino for her help in preparing the visuals for the book;

- Sam Scully for his careful reading and wise comments;
- The staff of the Archives of the University of Victoria, especially Nadica Lora, for the numerous ways in which they helped;
- Nikoo Najand for assistance in researching the history of the college and the early years of the university;
- The 160 people I interviewed for the project. The tapes of these interviews will be deposited in the UVic Archives for the use of people interested in UVic's history;
- The staff of McGill-Queen's University Press, particularly Adrian Galwin, for his wise stewardship, Joanne Muzak for her valuable suggestions and careful editorial work, Susanne McAdam and Garet Markvoort for their work on the visual dimensions of the book;
- Robert Sharp for his assistance in understanding student life of Victoria College;
- The staff of the Provincial Archives of British Columbia and the Vancouver Public Library for assistance in locating photographs;
- Elizabeth Coey, who assisted throughout, recalled much from her years at UVic, helped greatly with the editing, and did as much as was humanly possible to keep me organized.

Ian MacPherson
Victoria
October 2011

REACHING OUTWARD AND UPWARD

PROLOGUE

People have been studying, teaching, and learning in Gordon Head, where the University of Victoria now stands, for millennia. For the Coast and Straits Salish peoples, transmitting knowledge was central to their existence – understanding intimately the world around them was essential for the good life they enjoyed.

Despite the efforts of residential schools to obliterate that understanding, it has been transmitted across generations. It is concerned with knowledge about local places, land, plants, forest animals, and water life, the kinds of understandings that can only come from a sustained, intimate, and respectful connection to the land. It provides reflections on those larger questions that invariably perplex human beings: where do we come from, what is the meaning of life, how do we relate to nature, what constitutes justice, how do we resolve differences, treat ailments, and meet spiritual needs. The individuals and families who mastered such knowledge, the elders of whatever age, were revered, as they are to this day. Their insights should be reflected upon, particularly by people who speed by or who consume rather than engage the natural world they are given in trust.

But perhaps those of us who do not come from Indigenous backgrounds could learn most from their efforts to create holistic understandings of life. One should not impose impossible standards on all Indigenous people and expect that they all adhered perfectly to how they said they wanted to live. One must respect, though, the way in which so many, amid the hardships of the last 170 years, have sought to do so. Their constancy is impressive, their vision salutary. We can also learn from the awe evident within Indigenous knowledge, the recognition that human beings seek, and must seek, to understand so much more than they already know, so much that ultimately may not be knowable. At the very least, it will help us to become less certain about what we think we know.

Until recent years, Indigenous knowledge was not widely known, partly as a result of needing to resist efforts to obliterate it and partly because of the way it was pushed aside as settlement occurred. Fortunately, the situation is changing and Indigenous people are generously sharing more of their knowledge – but that is a matter for later chapters, much later chapters …

The Songhees Reserve, near downtown Victoria, 1906. Provincial Archives of British Columbia, F-09956.

1

....

ORIGINS

It was not an overwhelmingly obvious place for a university but it was promising. The Legislative Buildings had been completed in 1897, six years earlier, replacing the "Birdcages," the highly unusual buildings that had served legislators, public servants, and the city of Victoria for some forty years. In that year, 1903, the Canadian Pacific Railway started regular sailings between the city and Vancouver on the *Princess Victoria*, destined to become a coastal icon. So too would be the hotel the CPR commissioned Francis Rattenbury to design to front the James Bay tidal flats. When completed in 1908, it would be called the Empress. Out on the nearby Saanich Peninsula, Jennie Butchart was thinking about starting a flower garden at the bottom of an ugly limestone quarry; in time, too, it would grow to become an icon and international tourist attraction.

A talented group of architects, most prominently Rattenbury and Samuel Maclure, were constructing remarkable public and private buildings, many of them the architectural glories of their time. A century later, they still are. Everywhere, it seemed, there was development and construction. A small city of 30,000 in 1903, Victoria was vibrant, proud, and confident.

There could still be vestiges of a "frontier" town, however, when large numbers of workers from the sea, forests, and mines wandered its streets. In reality, though, the old order was passing. The influence of Hudson's Bay Company was fading. Indigenous peoples, once commonly found on the city's streets, were now rare. The Songhees were retreating to their View Royal reserve, their numbers ravaged by disease – down from an estimated 8,500 fifty years earlier to a few hundred. The Esquimalt and Tsartlip peoples were similarly shadows of what they had been. It was the great, often overlooked, tragedy of Victoria's early years.

For its size, Victoria was remarkably cosmopolitan. It was on an island but it wasn't insular. Ships from many countries could be regularly found in its harbour. Whaling and sealing industries were still important. Victoria's hinterland stretched along the BC coast and into the Bering Sea. On the west coast, only San Francisco had a busier port. It was, however, changing rapidly. Immigrants from some of Britain's "more elevated" classes (or reputed to be) tried to cast a cloak of gentility over the city. A few were the celebrated "remittance men," despatched to the "colonies" by their families (from whom they received regular allowances or "remittances") for having misbehaved or so as to dampen sibling rivalry.

From the mid-nineteenth century onward, the Victoria harbour was a busy place, as this photo from ca. 1925 suggests. Provincial Archives of British Columbia, D-5499.

Most of the population, however, belonged to the working class, clustered in neighbourhoods fanning out from the central core. The most obvious were 3,000 Chinese, clustered in "Chinatown," a small area along Fisgard and adjoining streets. Others came from the slums of industrialism or the limited rural opportunities in turn-of-the-century British Isles. There was a significant Japanese population, associated primarily with fishing and gardening businesses, and several other minority groups – Jews, Germans, and Ukrainians – drawn by the possibilities of the "new" land. Numerically, though, the largest contingent came from other parts of Canada. They brought with them economic connections, institutional loyalties (to churches and fraternal organizations), and social views that would help shape the city, including how and why a university might be developed.

In 1903 Victoria, the face of the city was being transformed. Streetcars were replacing omnibuses. Three radial rail lines stretched northward into the Saanich Peninsula and one eastward into Oak Bay. Cars were more frequent on the city streets. Classical music, opera, and live theatre, performed by talented local amateurs and touring professionals, could be found. The Searchlight Theatre featured the latest magic lantern shows. R.E. Gosnell, the legislative librarian, was scheming to create a provincial archives. The specimens collected by the Provincial Museum since 1889 overflowed its quarters in the Colonial Administration Building. There was a sprinkling of writers and artists. Clive Phillips Woolley, a very popular writer at the time despite or perhaps because of his strongly racist views, had just departed Oak Bay for an island off the Saanich Peninsula. Robert Service worked in a bank on Government Street, his poetic skills largely unknown. The Victoria Public Library was planning a new and imposing edifice, funded by the Carnegie Foundation. There was a literary society, an operatic society, an historical society, and a horticultural society. There was a fashionable elite identified by wealth, attachments to the old country and, increasingly, affiliations with Canada beyond the Rockies. There was much that was positive in Victoria in 1903. It was a bustling community caught up in the great transitions then sweeping Canada's urban places.

There were, however, reasons for concern. Across the straits, Vancouver was becoming the province's metropolis.

Chinatown as it existed, probably about 1900. Provincial Archives of British Columbia, D-04748.

Government Street, one of the city's main commercial streets, stretching northward from Fort Street, ca. 1900. Provincial Archives of British Columbia, B-03703.

Since 1886, when the first train had arrived, steady streams of people, ideas, and economic opportunities flowed in from the East. Its hinterland stretched across the province and into the Prairies. It was sustained by produce from the rich soils of the Fraser River Valley and by bountiful harvests from the sea. It possessed a remarkably capable economic elite. It was a formidable competitor for Victoria in an age of unrestrained, ruthless urban boosterism. Its leaders never doubted that their city should be the dominating force in the province, culturally, intellectually, and economically. They assumed that any provincial university would be located there.

According to UVic's historian Peter Smith, Victorians first expressed interest in developing a "provincial university" in the 1870s, just after confederation with Canada.[1] It was premature: the city then had only 4,000 residents and the province lacked funds. By the early 1880s, however, Victoria had 14,000 people, and the province was enjoying a boom period. Victoria High School, by then a decade old, had over 100 students, many of them wanting to attend university after graduation. Leaders from the high school and the community, joined by school board trustees, prominent city leaders, and the *Colonist* (one of the city's main newspapers), promoted the formation of a university, only to be thwarted by a municipal council worried about potential costs.

In 1888, the *Colonist* and high school leaders forcefully pushed the idea, leading the provincial government to pass enabling legislation in 1890. The government somewhat spinelessly left it to a "senate" consisting of all university graduates in the province to decide when and where it would be developed. The result, as described in great detail by Smith, was a vigorous competition between Victoria and Vancouver, each with about the same number on the "senate."

The university dream gathered slow momentum over the next fifteen years. Then a willing partner appeared: McGill University, which was basking in a "golden age" built on the intellectual strengths of Montreal, strong associations with British and American universities, and a remarkable group of academics in the sciences and social sciences. McGill was dreaming of forming a national university with affiliated colleges spread all across the country.

Negotiations proceeded quickly but, as it turned out, only Vancouver was ready to respond. Its college opened in 1899, offering parts of the first two years of the McGill curriculum. Three years later, one of McGill's stellar faculty members, Henry Marshall Tory, came west to inspect that college and to investigate creating others. He speedily reached an agreement with the Victoria School Board, and in 1903 classes began. The roots of the University of Victoria had been established.

Victoria looking north from the Parliament Buildings. The stretch of water to the left is the Gorge, the location for many of the city's industrial and shipping businesses, ca. 1905. Provincial Archives of British Columbia, F-09652.

overleaf | In 1908, Rudyard Kipling wrote, "Amongst all the beautiful places in the world, and I think I have seen the most beautiful of them, Victoria ranks the highest." Perhaps this picture, showing an iconic view of Victoria, ca. 1930, demonstrates in part why he thought that way. Provincial Archives of British Columbia, B-07313.

2

....

BEGINNINGS

E.B. Paul, principal of Victoria College and Victoria High School, 1903–08; municipal inspector, 1908–20; principal of Victoria College, 1920–27. Picture taken in 1925.

When first built, they were the pride of many Canadian towns and cities. They were the high schools and collegiate institutes constructed in virtually every significant Canadian community from 1890 onward. In an age when only 3 per cent of the population went to universities, they were the main final educational destiny for many young people in the expanding middle class. They were usually large and impressive, often with classical columns and motifs, monuments to the importance and solemnity of knowledge, and conspicuous legacies of the civic leaders of the times.

In 1902, therefore, Victorians were proud when a new high school opened at the corner of Fort Street and Fernwood Road (site of the present Central Middle School). It was the third incarnation of Victoria High School, smaller versions having been built in 1876 and 1882. Designed by Francis Rattenbury, the high school cost the shocking amount of nearly $500,000 to build. The building had its critics, especially as problems appeared over time,[1] but it was badly needed. It was immediately full.

Seven more students, however, were squeezed in when classes opened in the autumn of 1903 – four young women and three young men. They were the students of the first class of Victoria College, or, to give it its full name, "McGill University College of British Columbia situated at Victoria." Not everyone, most particularly loyal graduates of the University of Toronto, welcomed this Montreal intrusion. Some questioned the credentials of the instructors: all were teachers from Vic High, including the principal, Edward B. Paul. They were not paid. They taught demanding loads in English, French, Greek, Latin, mathematics, and physics. Their students were evaluated through final exams set and graded by McGill staff in Montreal. Fortunately, they performed well, starting a tradition of high academic achievement that would become the college's chief source of pride throughout it sixty-year existence.

College enrolments soon exceeded the space allotted to them in Paul's office. In 1907, a small, two-room building was constructed behind the school to house the students (and the high school typing class). It became known by various irreverent nicknames, including "the barn," the "chicken house," and the "wooden shack."[2]

It was a stopgap on the way to a provincial university. Some Victorians (not graduates of the University of Toronto) favoured helping McGill realize its national dreams, but most came to prefer creating a new provincial

left | Victoria High School, the first home for Victoria College, as it existed in 1902. Provincial Archives of British Columbia, B-03271.

right | The annex of Victoria High School in 1915, where classes of Victoria College were held from 1907 to 1914.

institution. The provincial government of Richard McBride ultimately agreed with them. In 1907, it passed the University Endowment Act, allocating proceeds from the sale of some two million acres of crown land to the establishment of a provincial university. In 1908, it passed an Act to Establish and Incorporate a University for the Province of British Columbia. The two acts precipitated intense, sometimes furious, debates between people in Victoria and Vancouver over where a university might be located. The government decided in favour of the brash urban upstart across the straits. In 1910, it set aside a large plot of "endowment lands" in Point Grey, to the west of Vancouver's urban core, for its development. The decision was not well-received in Victoria.

3

THE COLLEGE TRADITIONS

Academic institutions are most obviously concrete places – classrooms, libraries, laboratories, gymnasia, cafeterias, bike racks, and parking spots. They should also be places for beauty, where art, music, literature, and architecture – the gifts of talented people – are preserved, cultivated, and appreciated. Above all, though, they are places of the mind: locations for enquiry, analysis, and discussion; settings for relationships, experiences, and memory; environments for comprehension, growth, and wonderment. Their nature as concrete places is relatively easily understood. The artistic and intellectual impact is more difficult to evaluate.

Understanding the physical side of Victoria College's history means following somewhat undignified quests for controllable premises. The college vacated its first restricted premises behind the high school in 1914, joining the high school in new, impressive facilities at the corner of Fernwood and Grant Streets. Assigned most of the top floor, the college staff and forty students enjoyed space and pleasant views of the city when classes began in September 1915.

Their pleasure was brief. Midway through the academic year, the provincial government announced the opening of the University of British Columbia (UBC) in Vancouver and indicated that it would receive all the available post-secondary funding. Victoria College would be closed.

The decision, however, was not for the ages. In 1920, a steady stream of returning First World War veterans confronted bleak economic prospects amid a severe depression. Governments across Canada reacted by enabling more young people, especially veterans, to attend universities. It was the beginning of a century-long love affair with education in Canada; though, as with most love affairs, what it meant and how it would be financed was not immediately apparent.

Several prominent Victorians called for the reopening of the college. They included current and former mayors, the board of the high school, and the editors of both the *Colonist* and the *Victoria Times*, the city's most important newspapers. The key leader was E.B. Paul, the redoubtable former principal of Victoria High School (1892–1908) and of the College (1903–08). In 1919, he was the municipal inspector of schools and a member of the UBC convocation, which gave him the opportunity to influence many people – which he did. He was joined by S.J. Willis, his successor as college principal

The Second Year Arts Class of Victoria College, 1908–09. Front row: Erna Papke, Katie Coates, Jean Robinson. Middle row: Edna Lehman, Alice Corry, Nita McKillican, Jean Roberts, Winnifred Fox, Mamie Logan, Helen Luscombe, Mildred Ross. Back row: Albert Hartmen, Harold Eberts, R.F. Loenholm, Kenneth Drury, Harold Beckwith. Missing: Rena Chandler, Marshall Goderon, Mary Hamilton, Barbara Mowat.

(1908–15), and in 1919 the superintendent of education in the Department of Education. They were a formidable pair.

Often rancorous debates about the college's reopening took place within the UBC senate, on the Victoria School Board, in public places, and even on the floor of the BC Legislature. Finally, a somewhat beleaguered government agreed to reopen the college as an affiliate of UBC. In the autumn of 1920, six instructors welcomed some seventy-five students to rooms in the high school. This beginning was not particularly promising. The president of UBC, Leonard S. Klinck – the person ultimately responsible for the reopening – was pessimistic about "such a fragment of an institution."[1] A few prominent Victorians agreed, while others questioned whether the reopening could be afforded. Life would never be easy for the college.

The principal of the revived college was E.B. Paul, by then over seventy years old. Two of the six teachers came from the pre-1915 staff and two were former students. Collectively, they taught English (which somehow also counted as history!), Latin, Greek, French, chemistry, mathematics, physics, and philosophy. Like a Saturday movie serial at the Searchlight Theatre, the saga continued.

Within a few months, it was clear that co-habitation with the high school was unsatisfactory. Space was at a premium, and both institutions had strong-willed leaders – at least one more than was desirable. The search began for an alternative location, which was quickly found – Craigdarroch Castle, located in Rockland, one of the city's most prestigious districts. It would be the college's home for some twenty-five years.

It was a pretentious building – a "bonanza castle" – an imitation of the indulgences of the wealthy robber barons of the American railroad and mining industries. It had been built by Robert Dunsmuir, a Victoria resident who had grown wealthy from coalmines on Vancouver Island. From the outside, it was as grand an edifice as could be found at any Canadian college or university.

Inside, however, it was deteriorating, although vestiges would always remain of its original glory: stained glass windows, ornate fireplaces, oak panelling, large staircases, and grand balconies. There were appropriate inscriptions over the fireplaces: "Welcome ever smiles and farewell goes out sighing," a quotation from Shakespeare's *Troilus and Cressida*, and, "Reading maketh a full man," from Roger Bacon. Otherwise the interior was declining. Family feuds following Dunsmuir's death had meant it had not been well maintained before the castle and its adjoining land were sold to developers. They in turn raffled the castle away when they subdivided the property. In 1917, the interior of the castle was gutted to make way for hospital beds for returning wounded veterans. The college replaced those beds with basic classroom furniture when it took over in 1920.

Between 1920 and 1945, the college's enrolment varied between 180 and 200 students. It taught courses drawn from the first two years of the UBC Arts programme, though Commerce was added in 1930 because of community pressures and the onset of the Great Depression. It possessed a strong sense of community, though it cannot be said that everyone "belonged." The teachers formed a small and earnest cadre. Student-teacher bonds ran deep, particularly during the era of Percy Elliott, a physicist who served as principal from 1927 to 1943. A humane, pleasant, and disciplined man, Elliott embodied many of the personal virtues the college sought to inculcate in its students.

The students, almost all local, spent their days among people they already knew, most having graduated from local high schools. They came largely from comfortable middle-class homes, almost invariably Euro-Canadian, though a very few were from Chinese and Japanese-Canadian families. They had a vibrant social life and, for those who wished it, frequent political debates and ideological controversies.[2] Since most lived nearby, they could stay easily into the evening. Several would became prominent in later life: for example, Pierre Berton, the writer/journalist;[3] Jack Shadbolt, the artist; and several judges, good teachers, successful business people, and important public servants. The college fostered a strong theatrical tradition and a lively student journal. Each year, scores of students crossed the straits on what were called weekend "Invasions" (a term the crew of the *Princess Victoria* probably thought appropriate). Theoretically, the "Invasions" were organized for athletic competitions with UBC and other Mainland sports teams,

Craigdarroch Castle, as portrayed when it was still a residence for the Dunsmuir family. It seemed strangely out of place in what was still very much a frontier society, but it was (initially at least) a handsome abode for a college. Provincial Archives of British Columbia, B-04591.

left | He became known as a writer, but Pierre Berton as a student showed some talent as a cartoonist.

right | The *Victoria Princess*, the vessel used by Victoria College students when invading Vancouver. Vancouver Public Library, 2542.

but they also offered (by all reports) hours of exuberant partying before and during the voyages as well as between and after the sporting contests.

This rather pleasant existence disintegrated, at least in part, before the adversities of the Great Depression in the thirties, the outbreak of the Second World War in 1939, and the sudden death of Percy Elliott in 1943. Elliott's passing left a huge vacuum: in addition to his administrative responsibilities, he had lectured fourteen hours a week and had run a lab for another ten. The timing of his death coincided with major problems for the college: as war costs were mounting, the provincial government was reducing its financial support for the college. The College Council, its governing body, added to the woes: an awkward tripartite partnership involving UBC, the School Board, and the Department of Education, it could not name a successor to Elliott.

··· THE SPORTS OF VICTORIA COLLEGE ···

The student march on the Legislature in favour of moving Victoria College northward to share accommodations with the Normal School, 1946.

The provincial government was even uncertain about what the college's future should be. A Legislative Committee had just published a report on post-war reconstruction advocating the creation of junior colleges to provide vocational and technical training. Some in Victoria thought the college should be the first such institution – a view not popular at the college. One of its instructors, William Robbins, from the English Department, prepared a statement cogently mixing survey results with clear arguments on behalf of a "Liberal Arts" curriculum. It summarized well the commitments and beliefs of many college supporters, then, in the past – and in the future. It helped carry the day. The crisis passed. A new principal was appointed – John T. Ewing, an educational psychologist from the Victoria Normal School.

In 1946, another crisis emerged as returning veterans doubled the college's enrolment to some 600 students. They complained about insufficient classrooms, unsafe facilities, and overwhelmed instructors. On 10 October 1946, they organized one of the more unusual protests in Canadian university history. Several hundred strong, they joined with others in marching on the Legislature and other buildings downtown, including the premier's home. They carried banners with such messages as, "Into the Valley of Death Filed the 600," "A Castle for Dunsmuir – A Fire Trap for Us," and "Never Has So Little Been Denied So Few." One of their number, Reginald Roy (afterward a military historian at UVic), commented, "they marched in step"[4] – though by studying the pictures that have survived, it appears they needed some practice. Nevertheless, its somewhat military precision made it an unusual student protest, as student protests are usually noted more for enthusiasm than discipline.

The main purpose of the march was to advance the argument that the college should share space with the Victoria Normal School, located at the corner of Lansdowne and Richmond Roads, some two kilometres north of the castle. The site contained a large and splendid building (the Young Building), an attractive large house, and some other buildings – there was easily enough space for both institutions.

The march carried a petition bearing over 14,000 names favouring the union. An alarmed premier, John Hart, appointed a committee the next day to investigate the request. Rather remarkably, six days later, it recommended

It was an ideal setting for a quiet Liberal Arts college – the Lansdowne campus in 1954. Provincial Archives of British Columbia, I-23089.

above | The library in 1948, the centre of Victoria College's intellectual life – and a Liberal Arts education. Provincial Archives of British Columbia, I-0187.

facing page, above | Harry Hickman, French scholar, outstanding teacher, principal of Victoria College (1952–63), and stalwart contributor to UVic in its earliest years.

facing page, below | Gordon Head was a military base that included sophisticated radio intelligence operations directed at the Japanese, the rehabilitation of prisoners of war, and casualty retraining as well as the training of officers. Here some soldiers pose in a captured Japanese Kurogane scout car in January 1944. Provincial Archives of British Columbia, I-51845.

that the college move in to the Normal School. It did – within a week. On 15–16 November, teachers and students (seventeen of them hired to do the heavy work) marched north carrying books, lab equipment, and furniture to the college's new premises.

The college would remain on the Lansdowne campus for some seventeen productive years. Its curriculum gradually expanded, particularly in the social sciences and sciences. It hired some instructors with advanced degrees and research interests. The mostly local student population swelled to nearly a thousand. Some, such as Ian Tyson, from nearby Cadboro Bay, attended while they worked out what to do with their lives. In his case, he attended only briefly before leaving to become a folk singer and balladeer for North America's disappearing "cowboy culture."[5] Others, some of whom spent long hours mastering the intricacies of bridge in the basement of the Young Building, found different kinds of employment, the college also having served them as a place for self-discovery, not the least contribution post-secondary institutions make.

In retrospect, the college seems idyllic, set in ancient groves of Garry oaks, offering splendid views of the Olympic Mountains and, in time, carefully cultivated flower and shrub gardens. It possessed a quietly serious quality about it, based on the common assumptions of the Canadian academic world at the time. Intellectually it reflected a stream of mingled intellectual perceptions increasingly referred to as the Liberal Arts. Its curriculum included a changing collection of writers, dramatists, and scientists, mostly male, drawn overwhelmingly from the North Atlantic world. Though not specifically religious (unlike many other Canadian colleges, it did not teach theology), its purview was solidly within the Judeo-Christian tradition. It encouraged the study of science but less so than the humanities. It emphasized writing skills and the organized presentation of ideas but also the building of "character." It was more interested in past knowledge and opinion than in contemporary findings and insights. It provided a good preparation for teaching, law, medicine, and the public service – the career choices of many in attendance.

Some students flourished in that environment. Three became Rhodes Scholars, several won gold medals at UBC, and many prospered in UBC honours programmes. In 2008, over forty of them, all having had distinguished careers, would prepare a thoughtful and thankful book about their experiences.[6]

The college nevertheless encountered problems in the decade that began in 1946. Co-habitation with the Normal School was problematic. The two principals, John Ewing of the college and H.O. English of the Normal School, feuded constantly – their disagreements are well-examined in Peter Smith's history. At one point, they only communicated by typed messages though their offices were virtually adjoining. The tensions, however, did not seem to affect either the student experience or faculty members very much. Mountain top storms do not always affect the valleys.

In the mid-1950s, the provincial government decided that its two normal schools (in Vancouver and Victoria) should become Faculties of Education. It decreed that the Victoria Normal School should be amalgamated with Victoria College, a decision that created considerable anxiety on the Lansdowne campus. The initial apprehensions abated, though they did not entirely disappear, when Harry Hickman from the college's French Department, was appointed principal. He was a remarkably tactful and highly respected colleague, greatly assisted by two other peacemakers – the mathematicians Bob Wallace from the college and Hugh Farquhar from the Normal School, three men whose peacemaking skills would make remarkable contributions to UVic.

The quieting of the tensions under Hickman came just in time. Other deeply significant issues were emerging, including the recurrent debate over the college's future. In the community, many prominent citizens advocated forming a full-fledged university. They included Joseph Clearihue, a member of the first college class in 1903, William Mearns (who lived in Vancouver but had attended the college in the 1920s), the Victoria Chamber of Commerce, local media celebrities, several senior civil servants, the local member of the Legislative Assembly, the city council, and George Pearkes, the local member of Parliament and soon to be lieutenant-governor.

That alternative, however, was not a foregone conclusion. UBC did not want an independent rival. Some on campus and in the community wanted the status quo to continue, especially when the college gained the right to grant degrees as a UBC affiliate in 1962. The controversies of some forty years earlier were resurfacing. They would echo from 1956 to 1963.

Another complicated issue abetted them: the struggle for suitable space. Efforts to add land owned by the Hudson's Bay Company (HBC) adjoining the Lansdowne campus proved futile. Attention then turned to 120 acres located about two kilometres away, half owned by the federal government and half by the HBC. During the war, it had been a military training base and there were some forty barracks on it that were still useful.

Looking up to where UVic would emerge: the view from Cadboro Bay. UVic would rise on the hills above the Cadboro Beach Hotel, long a popular place for day trips and pleasant evenings for people in Victoria. Photo courtesy of Provincial Archives of British Columbia, A-02977.

The decision to purchase the land, as described by Smith, was controversial because of uncertainties over funding and questions about where the university would be best located. The debates ended in 1959 when the College Council purchased the land for the then considerable sum of $100,000. It was a particularly bold, even courageous, action for the board to take.

The purchase precipitated an extensive fundraising campaign. The provincial government, heavily lobbied by leading Victorians, offered to match donations to create a capital fund of some $3,000,000 (subsequently raised to $5,000,000). Many faculty and students as well as key leaders in Victoria rallied to the campaign, making it a cause that "thoroughly united the whole community."[7] Donating families became known as "university founders." Students voluntarily canvassed nearby neighbourhoods for contributions. Within less than five years the target had been reached, helping to convince the premier, W.A.C. Bennett, that a university in Victoria made sense. He announced one would be developed when he opened one of the first buildings constructed on the Gordon Head lands in January 1963, a building named after Joseph Clearihue.

The college ended, therefore, as it had existed – amid extensive debates over purpose and location. The college's closing, though, did not end its influence. Its traditions would long influence the university that succeeded it, especially its emphasis on a Liberal Arts curriculum, strong commitment to good teaching, convivial staff relationships, a steadily broadening curriculum, an aggressive administration, and strong community relations. They provided a constructive basis for the university, which (after some debate) was named the University of Victoria. The odyssey that had started some sixty years earlier in a high school principal's office was finally over.

Depositing the results of the UVic building campaign in the early 1960s. The fund treasurer, E.D.B. Henshaw, and Betty Beecroft depositing two million dollars into a vault at the Canadian Imperial Bank of Commerce as guards John Jones (left) and Stanley Connors (right) look on. Unfortunately, it was not enough to meet the demands, especially since UVic had to purchase the land on which it would sit.

יהי אור

MULTITUDO SAPIENTIUM SANITAS ORBIS

left | The motto and coat of arms of the University of Victoria were the result of the enthusiasms of Principal E.B. Paul, who enlisted the help of local heraldic enthusiast, Albert J. Hill, in creating Victoria College's coat of arms shortly after its formation in 1903. Slightly modified, the coat of arms was registered in 1961 and became UVic's coat of arms when the university was formed on 1 July 1963. The motto over the torch's flame means "Let there be light" in Hebrew; the bottom banner translates from Latin as, "A multitude of the wise is the health of the world."

facing page | The flag of the University of Victoria. The three martlets (sometimes called dickey birds) at the top of the flag come from the coat of arms of McGill University and mark its early association with Victoria College.

The Victoria College Song

Hail to Alma Mater sing, hail to thee, Victoria!
Loudly now our praises ring, ring for thee, Victoria!
Standing proud on rocky highland,
Beacon of Vancouver's Island –
Singing Yeh-hee Ah-oor! Singing Yeh-hee Ah-oor!

Martlets red on argent field, memories of old McGill;
Open book on azure shield, symbols of our faith & will:
Hold we high the torch of learning
Seven flames forever burning
Singing Yeh-hee ah-oor! Singing Yeh-hee ah-oor!

Vikings fight on every field, play the game with spirits high!
Vikings fight and never yield, push right through and make that try!
Play it hard your laurels earning –
Near-defeat to vict'ory turning –
Singing Yeh-hee ah-oor! Singing Yeh-hee ah-oor!

– Dr Rodney Poisson. Source: http://spcoll.library.uvic.ca/
schoolnet/digicol/vic-col/vclv5/song.html

4

....

CONTEXTS

During the 1950s and 1960s, Canadians began to expect more from their universities. In 1951, the Massey Royal Commission on the Arts, Letters, and Sciences warned that inadequate financial investments and materialistic priorities were undermining the fundamental purposes of Canadian universities. It appealed for more support from governments and from the public. The appeal was heard. Federal as well as provincial governments increased their support for universities significantly.

The need for increased university support became clearer, too, in October 1957, when the Soviet Union launched *Sputnik 1*, the first Earth-orbiting artificial satellite. As it rose so did alarm in the United States. It spilled over into Canada. The Canadian government built the "Diefenbunker" in Ottawa so leaders could huddle should nuclear attack occur – and two lesser bunkers in Nanaimo and Nanoose Bay on Vancouver Island for their west coast counterparts. More importantly, *Sputnik 1* convinced governments that they should spend more money on scientific training and research at universities.

There were other pressures. During the 1960s, books such as George Grant's *Lament for a Nation* stoked Canadian nationalism. Some academics became alarmed over the Americanization of Canadian universities. They were concerned about what they saw being researched and taught, especially in the social sciences and humanities. Universities, they argued, had to create specifically Canadian curriculum, developed and taught by Canadians.

Then there were the baby boomers – the children born as veterans returned home after the war. Their maturing had convulsed elementary and secondary schools during the 1950s. They would soon be descending on the universities creating demands that could not easily be met.

UVic was born amid these concerns. It was not born alone. From St John's in Newfoundland to Victoria on Vancouver Island, provincial politicians, academics, parents, and civic leaders clamoured for more universities. Between 1959 and 1970, governments created fourteen universities across Canada, meaning new campuses, expanded research capacities, and more professors. In several instances – such as Calgary, Regina, Brandon, Winnipeg, Laurentian, Windsor, Université de Québec à Montréal, and Moncton as well as Victoria – colleges and/or normal schools were transformed into universities. It made some sense: college buildings, though

facing page | The site of UVic. The land owned by the Department of National Defence has been cleared, once used for farming, then converted to become the military base. The land owned by the Hudson's Bay Company is covered with (mostly) second growth forest. Most of the buildings in the pictures were barracks for the troops, who numbered over 800 when the base was in full use.

rarely entirely adequate, were available; many college/normal school staff members could teach university courses; some were engaged in research; and there were significant components of university support systems available – registrar's offices, classrooms, gymnasia, libraries. That did not mean the transition would be easy. Invariably there would be institutional cultural change, especially for those carrying on from the colleges, and developing the appropriate infrastructure would be difficult.

UVic faced all these challenges and would deal with them in its own way. It would respond to increasing concerns about Canadian intellectual life. It would expand, sometimes with remarkable speed, its research and teaching activities. It would be affected by the Cold War and international trends. It would face considerable turmoil, somewhat jarringly so in the tranquility of Victoria.

There was another contextual challenge – how to plan for the development of UVic. Martin Segger from the UVic Fine Arts Faculty, and a scholar interested in UVic and Victoria architecture generally, has explored this issue. He has described the process of thinking about and designing a university – not the easiest but certainly an interesting task – as follows.

THE CAMPUS PLAN

By early 1961 it was obvious Victoria College Council was in a quandary over whether to proceed with further expansion at the Lansdowne campus or go for a much more ambitious, and visionary, scheme at Gordon Head. Combining funds from all sources the Council anticipated a war chest of about $11.4 million to spend on capital development. It was at that point that Richard Biggerstaff Wilson, chair of the fundraising arm of the College, took matters in hand. Wilson was convinced the outside expert advice of world-class caliber was needed. On their own hook, Wilson and colleague Ernie Arnott flew down to San Francisco to interview William W. Wurster, at that time Dean of the School of Environment Design at University of California, Berkeley, and principal of the leading California architectural and planning group, Wurster, Bernardi & Emmons. Wurster and Don Emmons returned the visit, spending six days in Victoria. They immediately recommended moving the entire campus to Gordon Head in anticipation of 10,000 students.

Wurster, Bernardi & Emmons (WBE) were confirmed as consulting planners and they brought with them a strong design team, including one of America's foremost landscape planners, Lawrence Halprin, and educational planner Alfred W. Baxter. This group worked closely with local campus architects Robert Siddall & Associates to develop an overall campus plan and articulate design programs for individual buildings. By the end of the year the College had consolidated 140 acres at Gordon Head (to be expanded to 340 acres with further acquisitions by the end of 1964).

The resulting *Master Plan for the Development of the Gordon Head Campus* dated 17 December 1962 confirmed this overall strategy and set the tone, guidelines and direction for the university's growth over the next fifty years.

The WBE plan envisioned a destination university and a residential campus, walkable and livable. A core academic focus on an open quad would be contained within a ring road for vehicular access. The "Ring" actually named "University Drive" would be a circle of 2,000 feet (610 metres) in diameter, containing seventy-two acres (twenty-nine hectares). This would comprise the core academic uses: Liberal Arts to south, sciences to north, focusing on the open landscaped quadrangle. Outside the circle pedestrian and vehicular transport would link to services: residential, recreational, leisure, and utilitarian via this same ring road.

WBE brought more than just planning expertise. Wurster was a leading Bay Area pioneer of West Coast Modern, a design philosophy that eschewed the functional monumentalism of the International Style in favour of generating architectural form and style from building site and local context. In fact, he was an early proponent of what today we might call environmental design. Under WBE oversight, local Victoria architects would design the required campus buildings under a scheme that encouraged individual expression utilizing a shared pallet of materials, colours and textures. The dominant theme however would be the landscape itself, a garden setting which would both articulate and unite the ground plan with the buildings.

This philosophy was best articulated finally in the 1968 document entitled *Landscape Concept – University of Victoria* penned by Vancouver landscape architect John Lantzius who had articled with Halprin in San Francisco. One can discern Halprin's guiding hand in formulating the guiding principles of the campus architecture:

It has been our intent from the beginning to reflect the native plant material of Vancouver Island on the campus, and to create an imaginative environment using such plants as Garry Oak, Arbutus, Dogwood and other conifers. The major tree framework – which binds the buildings and open areas into a unified composition – is the most important and must receive the most

The architectural presentation drawing of what UVic might look like – by Alan Edwards. Special Collections, UVic Library, U000.5.2.

emphasis. This tree framework of evergreen trees (broadleaf and conifers) will be used primarily, in mass, to frame vistas, soften the architectural elements, as backgrounds, and as extensions of the forest areas ... The open areas will be contoured lawns which merge into the native forest.

With the brief exception of three years of Erickson & Massey as consulting planners (1967–70) under WBE's forty-six year consulting mandate, these principles have continued as the central objectives of the campus plan.[1]

5

STABILIZING YEARS, 1963–1975

Thomas Shanks McPherson, whose bequest made possible the library named after him and helped UVic through a difficult financial period in its history.

In 1963, the year the University of Victoria opened, a young American poet/songwriter wrote the song "The times they are a-changin'." It became something of an anthem for the times. It is not known whether Bob Dylan ever visited Gordon Head, but his song applied to the lands on which UVic rose. At first glance, the most obvious changes were physical. Chris Petter, now head of Special Collections in the UVic library, was a student that year. He recalls, "there wasn't much there. It wasn't much more than a former army camp with a few buildings on it. It was very barren ... It was a pretty wild country."[1] Ruts and poorly-filled trenches could be found on the portions of the land primarily used by the military. Second growth forests covered some of the land, generally that which was once owned by the Hudson's Bay Company. Some roads were unpaved. Fields were unkempt. A grove of academe it was not.

As the new buildings went up and army huts became classrooms, offices, and storage places, the university took shape. The land became manicured, although progress was slow: a subterranean stream turned much of it into swamps during the rainy periods that occur more often than most Victorians readily admit. Some buildings flooded frequently. The newly constructed building named for Joseph Clearihue became popularly known as ss *Clearihue* (for naval veterans, HMCS *Clearihue*) – its basement had to be drained so often by Island Tug and Barge. In time, however, a satisfactory drainage system was installed. Grass, shrubs, and flowers were planted. The future began to appear.

In 1964, the university opened a new library – the McPherson Library, named in honour of its benefactor, Thomas Shanks McPherson, a Victorian merchant and real estate developer. When he died in December 1962, he left $2,250,000 (plus some real estate investments) to the then-anticipated University of Victoria. The donation was particularly welcomed because the provincial government was not providing the university with all the funding that it had earlier promised. Moreover, the university was forced to buy the land on which it was being built – unlike the two Vancouver universities, which were developed on lands donated by the government. UVic also faced financial pressures when a BC-wide fundraising drive for universities fell short of its goal, an unfortunate outcome that affected UVic proportionately more than the other two universities.[2] To meet the shortfall, UVic increased student fees in 1965. The students organized a protest march downtown, but

University of Victoria Alma Mater Society President Paul Williams leads a large group of students down Douglas Street protesting fees increase on 18 October 1965.

facing page, above left | The procession leaving the Student Union Building for the official opening of UVic in 1963, led by Hugh Farquhar, the acting president.

facing page, above right | A link to the past. In 1963, the first class of Victoria College, which started classes in September 1903, held a sixtieth anniversary reunion, coinciding with the opening of the University of Victoria. They were: Back row: Clifford Rogers, Joseph B. Clearihue, Frederic G.C. Wood. Front row: Miss Sara Spencer, Mrs Kate Pottinger Thompson, Miss Josephine Wollaston. One other member of the class, Lilian (Mowat) Godard, telephoned her good wishes from Ontario.

facing page, below | Students stage a "Tent-In" outside the Student Union Building to protest the lack of housing, September 1968.

the higher fees remained. The financial situation worsened as UVic grew more rapidly than expected. In 1963, there were 1,500 students; by 1967, there were 3,500. The problem was that their fees did not cover all the incremental costs.

The first three years were further complicated because classes were divided between the Lansdowne and Gordon Head campuses. Buses carried students and faculty to and fro, somehow making the trips within the ten-minute break between classes. These daily migrations ended on 7 April 1966, when students and faculty staged a "long march" – a one-mile stroll reminiscent of the march over forty years earlier from Craigdarroch to Lansdowne, except hardly anyone carried anything substantial.

Aside from the Education Faculty, the student body included more men than women, a pattern that (as at most Canadian campuses) would persist for thirty years. More students from outside Victoria were evident, particularly from the BC Interior. There were more from the Prairies and Eastern Canada. The first Pacific Asian students appeared, as did increasing numbers of Americans, mostly from nearby states.

The faculty more than doubled between 1963 and 1967, when it numbered 300. Some came from British Columbia, but more from other provinces (particularly Alberta and Ontario) and from the United States (notably Oregon and California). Still others, a prominent and vocal minority, came from the United Kingdom. By the late 1960s, the faculty was a diverse group, increasingly subdivided by disciplinary associations, varying backgrounds, and social interests. Like the student body, the faculty would never again be as homogeneous as it had been throughout the college years.

When the university opened, the core of the curriculum – its main way of knowing – remained the Liberal Arts tradition. The humanities were generally at its centre, though the sciences were quickly becoming more important – much of the early construction at UVic, in fact, was for laboratories. Almost immediately, however, the Liberal Arts focus became blurred as new courses and programmes were added. The intellectual life of the new university quickened – including in the ways suggested in the essential message of Bob Dylan's song. Some new faculty brought the issues dominating American campuses at the time – protests against the

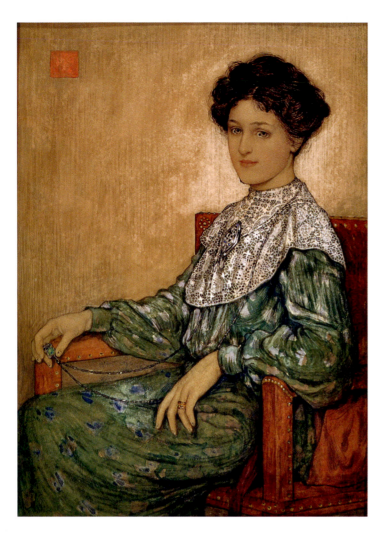

Katharine Maltwood (by Nico Jungman, 1905). The University of Victoria received the bequest of a Saanich house, art collections and an endowment from Katharine Maltwood on her death in 1961. The university built its collection largely on themes she had developed: the decorative and fine arts, particularly Western and Eastern porcelain, English furniture, European prints and drawings, modern and contemporary western Canadian art. Over the years, the UVic collection has grown to over 27,000 works of art.

In 1977 the university moved the museum and its collections to the University Centre on campus where it joined the University /continued on next page

Vietnam War, the civil rights/minority rights struggles, the challenging of materialism, and the angst of the baby boomers.

Many UVic students became fascinated with campus turmoil elsewhere – in the United States, other parts of Canada, and Europe. Through travel and reading they became fascinated with the questioning of traditional universities then sweeping campuses elsewhere. By the later 1960s, they were challenging what they were being taught and how UVic was being administered – though their protests were generally more civil than student protests elsewhere.

Some of the issues surfaced in noontime lectures by faculty and visitors, usually well attended since no classes were held at that time – a practice that regrettably disappeared as the university grew. They included talks by such prominent Canadians as John Diefenbaker, Jean Lesage, Charles Lynch, Laurier LaPierre, Tommy Douglas, and Walter Gordon. Several important international figures appeared, such as Linus Pauling, John Kenneth Galbraith, the civil rights leader James Meredith, (followed by the segregationist Alabama governor, George C. Wallace), Jerry Rubin, and Alexander Kerensky, the moderate, losing leader of the Russian Revolution.[3] UVic, though small and isolated, was not off the map.

UVic professors, however, presented most of the talks. Some were "engaged" academics concerned with contemporary social and political issues. A few were "performers" passionately addressing their favourite subjects – speakers who could "talk at great length in a very amusing and stimulating way."[4] Some promoted the "Free Speech" movement from California, insisting that students and faculty had the right – indeed, the obligation – to engage broad social, economic, and political issues.

Most of the speakers, though, spoke (often with equal passion) about more traditional academic concerns – literature, the Greek and Roman heritage, new science, art, culture, and history. Some promoted interdisciplinary experimentation, the new ways of knowing then shaping Simon Fraser University and some other universities. Speakers were also involved in campus symposia and weekend gatherings at Vancouver Island hotels. As Peter Smith later recalled those gatherings: "Never before or since can one recall such relaxed and open exchanges of opinion – much easier, no doubt, in a day when the average age differential between student and teacher was no more than ten or fifteen years. How wonderful it was to address the problems of the world with unrestrained good humour, in an atmosphere of trust and mutual respect. Student-faculty fraternization would continue and even intensify in the stormy years that lay ahead, but the process became more cliquish and covert."[5]

Some faculty members, particularly Roger Bishop and Carl Hare in the English Department, organized theatrical productions, the beginning of a

continued from previous page/
Collection of Canadian Art founded by Victoria College principal Dr Harry Hickman in 1953. In 2000, UVic received a major bequest from the estate of Michael Williams. It included many examples of fine and historic decorative and contemporary art and a substantial endowment that made possible the opening of the university's downtown "Legacy Art Gallery" as well as a Fine Arts Legacy Chair in Curatorial Studies of Modern and Contemporary Arts the Pacific Northwest (adapted from a larger text kindly provided by Martin Segger).

above | There have always been strong connections between UVic and the Victoria arts community. The artist Myfawnwy Pavelic was a part of that connection, especially in the 1960s and 1970s. Many of her paintings came to the Maltwood Gallery and can be found in many places around the university. A superb portraitist, she painted some of her friends who were important in the city's art community. Above is a painting of the "Limners," a group of eighteen artists who formed a loose coalition in Victoria during the 1960s and 1970s. It is a playful look at the group. University of Victoria Art Collections, U993.7.122.

A second painting by Myfawnwy Pavelic (at left) is of Pat Martin Bates, a member of the Limners and a long-time professor in the Faculty of Fine Arts. A third (at right) is of Robin Skelton, also from the Faculty of Fine Arts and a powerful voice among the Limners – not to mention UVic. University of Victoria Art Collections, U982.11.4 and U984.27.1.

rich tradition at UVic. Others encouraged creative writing on campus. They included the charismatic Robin Skelton, an authority on Irish literature, a poet, a highly skilled literary editor, and in his private (but well-known) life, a Wiccan of considerable renown. Still others joined talented students and members of the community to forge a strong music programme.

Students enjoyed a very rich extra-curricular life. From 1964 onward there were special "pub nights" in the Student Union Building (SUB) and gatherings on any evening in a very popular pub, the "Snug," in a nearby hotel. By the early 1970s, a permanent pub had been opened in the SUB. In time, it would be called Felicita's, after Felicita Gomez, a longtime janitor. Students could also view international film beginning in 1971, when Cinecenta, the student cinema/theatre, started showing films in classrooms. In 1975, it moved to is permanent home in the SUB. Students enjoyed Victoria, which, despite its reputation as a restful place for seniors, has always catered to the pleasures of the young. More than at other universities, students participated in various sports on a recreational or intercollegiate level. They joined numerous clubs devoted to serious academic pursuits and social issues or to relaxation, from skiing to chess. It was not an "evening campus" in the beginning, but the days were lively; entertaining one's self was easy, the serious study of the performing arts and spontaneous examinations of culture and thought flourished.

The opening of a new university, even one rising from the ashes of another institution, is usually an exciting period of anticipation, visioning, and creation. The boundaries of what is possible seem distant. That was certainly true of UVic, and to some extent its leaders must be given considerable credit.

The first president, G. "Harry" Hickman, was "acting." An engaging and modest, but strict man, devoted to French culture and literature, he pioneered in establishing language programmes, a commitment that took on added meaning in the separatist crisis of the 1960s. His work took him into Greater Victoria, as did that of many of his colleagues. From the beginning, UVic developed strongly within the context of its supportive communities.

The first "permanent" president was Malcolm G. Taylor, who arrived in the autumn of 1964. He was by training a political scientist, a useful background since there were some significant negotiations with governments to be concluded. He was also a veteran of the birthing period of the University of Calgary, when it was struggling beneath the heavy shadow cast by the University of Alberta – not unlike UVic in its relationship with UBC. He understood many of the problems confronting "emerging universities": planning the future with limited guidance from the past; establishing basic funding and administration systems; working with governments; constructing

Felicita Gomez, a very popular cleaning person who was honoured by having the students name their pub "Felicita's" in her name.

classroom/laboratory/office buildings; competing for faculty; and finding the balance between developing research and sustaining good teaching.

Taylor became an important transitional figure during his time as president (1964–68). He supported the Liberal Arts tradition and stressed the importance of teaching but also argued (perhaps somewhat contradictorily) for a multi-faceted university. He stressed the importance of marine biology, public administration, and Pacific connections – all of which emphasized the west coast context. He suggested stressing early British Columbian history and the "rich Indian [sic] tradition of the Pacific coast."[6] He promoted health studies, not easy because of how UBC guarded its medical programmes. He encouraged graduate programmes.

Taylor and UVic faced unique challenges. One of them emanated from the administrative practices and traditions of the college, traditions that arguably were maintained longer than they should have been. The college had always had to cope with uncertainty and varying pressures from enrolments, and they did so by giving department "heads," as they were then called, considerable freedom in making appointments. At the same time, the Normal School reflected the high school tradition of giving principals considerable power. That tradition included maintaining discipline, an open-ended responsibility, the overall, centralized management of schools, direct supervision of teachers, close following of curriculum, and control over teaching methods. One can hardly imagine an approach more out of step with evolving ideas about university administration during the 1960s.

In the last years of the college and in the early years of the university, several academic departments were created. Two of the most important departments, and two that particularly had to appoint teachers on short notice, were English and history. Their two "heads" – "chairmen" would not have been accurate and the then-incumbents would have been offended if called "chairs" – were Roger Bishop and Sidney Pettit, respectively. Though reporting to others in the administration, they clearly "ran" their departments. They warred with each other over whatever funds were available, especially if connected to the library. Their struggles became legendary. They appointed whom they liked from among those they believed could teach effectively. They did not follow well-established hiring and promotion procedures – though, in their defence, the college and UVic had few set policies on such matters. Other departments followed similar practices, their heads also tending towards autocratic practices. It was not an administrative style that could long survive.

Another source for disquiet was a continuing and often heated debate over the university's essential purpose. The Liberal Arts tradition, as it was then widely conceived, emphasized deep familiarity with revered texts and highly disciplined ways of interpreting them. At their best, devoted Liberal

Arts scholars would immerse themselves in the writings of "great thinkers," reflecting carefully and at length upon them. Many such scholars developed into wonderful, even legendary teachers, communicating knowledge from great minds of the past and the few contemporaries who could pass muster. They demanded careful attention to consistent and logical thought from their students. Though there were exceptions, they rarely engaged in new and original research activities, as were becoming practiced in other parts of the academy at the time. Nor did they address many social and economic issues, except indirectly, and they were not always aware of their own biases, derived from culture, history, and gender. These limitations, but, even more, the advances in other ways of knowing, would soon create challenges and controversies. The times they were a-changin'.

Many of the strongest advocates of the Liberal Arts tradition, particularly in the English and other humanities departments, advocated creating colleges on the UVic campus. They did not want so much to imitate college systems of older British or American universities, as they were interested in counteracting the kind of increasing anonymity found on many university campuses by the 1960s. Students enrolled in the colleges could register in courses across the campus, but they would also participate in college life, take meals (including, perhaps, "high tables"), and attend talks, seminars, and occasions specially designed to enrich their university life.

Two colleges were created at UVic during the late 1960s, Craigdarroch and Lansdowne, each with its own residence. Each had its own tutors with small budgets to make the desired atmosphere possible. The experiment did not work well and died out within a few years. It is very difficult to sustain academic experiments that differ so much from the mass experience of mainstream universities in Canada and the United States. Administrative leaders in UVic's early years, moreover, were not entirely convinced it was the best model to follow,[7] and their support was crucial to its survival. It was a noble experiment led by some very dedicated people, but it just didn't fit – in Victoria or (nearly) anywhere else in North America.

The rise of science on campus was a more permanent change. The study of the sciences was an integral part of Liberal Arts, but generally as part of a greater whole. As the science disciplines developed in North America during the 1950s and 1960s, however, they tended to erect strong disciplinary boundaries around themselves, based on their own special ways of knowing. Students studying sciences followed carefully designed, cumulative curricula that never seemed large enough for the scientists involved, let alone for enrolment in courses across the Liberal Arts. The scientists, too, were generally devoted to graduate programmes, an objective that clashed with those wanting to develop an exceptional undergraduate institution – the usual goal of most Liberal Arts advocates.

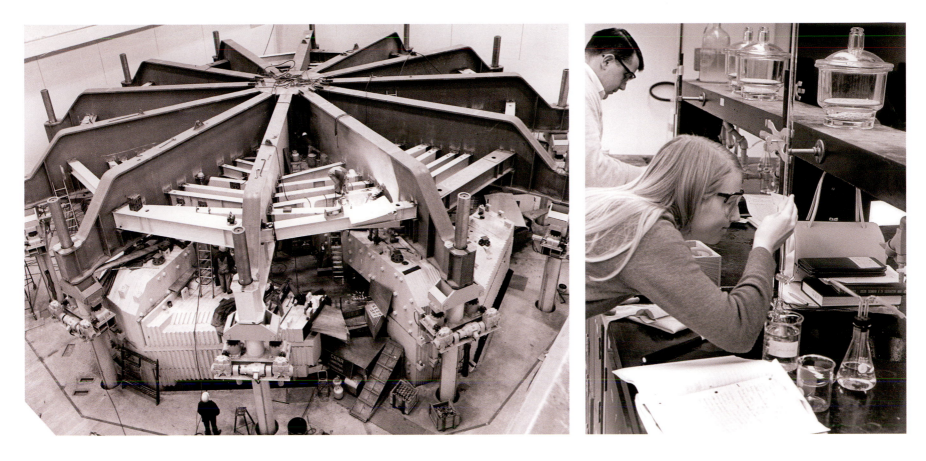

Almost immediately, the scientists prospered. In 1968, UVic physicists collaborated with colleagues at UBC and Simon Fraser (and shortly thereafter from the University of Alberta) to create TRIUMF (Tri-University Meson Facility), a subatomic physics laboratory housed at the University of British Columbia. It would become an outstanding example of interuniversity partnerships; in time, a national centre that included work on particle physics, molecular and materials science, and nuclear medicine.[8]

As the UVic science departments expanded during the 1960s and 1970s, they added many outstanding researchers. In contrast to researchers in the humanities and to a lesser extent the social sciences, scientists tend to conceptualize their research over longer periods and within elaborate intellectual frameworks. They based their work more on cumulative, incremental knowledge judged through international peer evaluation. They were in the vanguard (though they were not alone) in promoting the internationalization of research at UVic.

above, left | TRIUMF was one of the biggest science projects in the history of UVic. In this 1972 picture, the cyclotron on the UBC campus – where many UVic scientists undertook their most important research – is nearing completion, 1972.

above, right | Chemistry quickly became one of UVic's most important departments after 1963, undertaking extensive research and teaching many students. This picture shows students engaged in a titration experiment in an Elliott Building classroom, 1969.

facing page | Each term ended like this – writing exams in the old gym, 1965.

All of these characteristics, plus increased government funding for science, meant that UVic scientists attracted steadily larger research grants. They employed graduate students in significant numbers. They proudly demonstrated the immediate, practical value of what they did.

Researchers in other faculties pursued more eclectic, less cumulative ways of expanding knowledge. They had more difficulty demonstrating the practical, immediate significance of the research they undertook. The resultant divergence would create differences within the UVic campus as it did in many other universities. It was a local manifestation of a major issue for the Western world. In 1960, the British scientist and author C.P. Snow published a very powerful book, *The Two Cultures and the Scientific Revolution*, lamenting the growing split between sciences and other kinds of knowledge, particularly the humanities. He argued that only thoughtful exchanges between them would unleash the full potential of both. His message was not well absorbed, though his book was widely read at UVic and elsewhere. The modern world embraced the solutions that science offered, often without developing the social capacity to utilize them to the best effect.

There were other major changes at UVic during the 1960s and 1970s. Community pressures and emerging public needs led the university to develop the School of Nursing in 1966 and the School of Social Welfare (as the university originally called Social Work) in 1967. They marked an important shift away from the idea of a Liberal Arts university, but they were in keeping with the kind of multi-faceted university increasingly the norm all across Canada and the United States. They were significantly and directly affected by government policies and provincial priorities. They were driven, at least in part, by community needs, the requirements of professional organizations, and by experiences "in the field." They found much of their wisdom outside the controlled worlds of laboratories or the cloistered environment of libraries.

Shortly after the university came into being, the already strong traditions in theatre and music also led to the creation of a new faculty devoted to them and also to art. It was created in 1966. It possessed several colourful teachers and particularly enthusiastic students who disagreed frequently about how the faculty should develop. It was a very lively and creative faculty.

During UVic's early years the Normal School became a Faculty of Education. It grew steadily, partly because, in addition to serving schools on Vancouver Island, it taught many students from "beyond Hope," as they were colloquially called, because they came from the interior of the province to the east and north of the community of Hope. The faculty developed particularly strong ties with communities in the Okanagan and the Kootenays, in the process pioneering in the development of distance education at UVic.

··· SOME OF THE ARTS AT UVIC ···

The Education Faculty also embraced the university's growing commitment to research. It encouraged younger faculty without graduate degrees to pursue them. Several did so, particularly at the University of Oregon. It hired new faculty members as much for their research as their teaching qualifications. This shift in emphasis alarmed some older faculty who were concerned primarily with training students in classroom management and teaching skills. It was a cultural shift favouring the young and the new over the older – the ones who seemingly were being left behind.

Similar situations could be found elsewhere on campus. In English and mathematics some first-year instructors also taught in particularly demanding and time-consuming ways. They also taught well, their courses becoming one of the ways in which the university could be confident that its graduates met minimal standards of literacy and numeracy. They had little time – and perhaps interest – for research as it was becoming increasingly understood within the Canadian academy.

The university, however, was resolute. It expected younger faculty without graduate degrees to earn them, even providing them with "assisted leave" amounting to $1,500 a year ($1,200 if one was single!). While that sum seems trivial today, in the context of the time it represented about 20 per cent of an annual salary – a not ungenerous programme.

The shift in the research/teaching balance was one of the reasons for the undercurrent of discontent that was surfacing by the late 1960s. The other main reasons were inadequate procedures for appointment and reappointment and the lack of a sound tenure document. The waters around UVic might have looked calm but there were dangerous currents underneath.

Such issues were not unique to UVic. The development of new universities and the addition of thousands of new professors across the country highlighted, rarely positively, the employment practices of the Canadian academy. The Canadian Association of University Teachers (CAUT), formed in 1951, was created primarily because of their inadequacies. By the 1960s, it was overwhelmed by the cases that were cropping up almost everywhere, including Victoria.

In 1968, Malcolm Taylor resigned from the presidency, partly because of the controversies over employment practices – an "academic liberal," to use Peter Smith's phrase, he found the associated debates particularly painful.[9] Robert Wallace replaced him on an "acting" basis and would stay for a year. Like Harry Hickman at the time of the university's founding, Wallace was a healing figure. He possessed and maintained a reputation as an open, decent, and conciliatory person accumulated over more than thirty-five years of teaching at the college and the university.

Wallace gave way to the new president, Bruce Partridge, in September 1969. Partridge came from the mainstream of American universities,

Robert Wallace, student of Victoria College (1924–29), teacher of mathematics at Victoria College (1933–63), UVic administrator (1964–71), acting president (1968–69), chancellor (1972–78), pictured at his desk, not dated.

specifically the Johns Hopkins University, where he had
served as vice-president administration and treasurer.
From the beginning of his career, he had been attracted to
administrative work. Dynamic, forceful, and determined, he
was a strong advocate of research and of hiring only highly
qualified faculty members. He left little doubt as to where
he stood on appointment, promotion, and tenure decisions.
After a year of relative peace, the underlying personnel issues
erupted in the academic year, 1970–71. A number of difficult
cases (ultimately eighteen) emerged, fifteen concerning faculty renewal, three about tenure decisions. The uncertainties
caused by the inadequacies of the UVic process at the time –
and an understaffed administrative structure – were further
exacerbated by Partridge's strained relationship with the
dean of Arts at the time, John P. Climenhaga.[10] Partridge's
confident manner, clearly American in style, became
widely resented. When he denied tenure in three controversial cases, the pent-up pressures exploded. The Faculty
Association called emergency faculty meetings. Students
did the same, and sometimes 700 showed up. Comparisons
to the ferment at American and European universities were
made. When the Board of Governors tried to placate matters by calling a mass meeting to give its views, they had
little impact.

In January 1971, the student newspaper *The Martlet*,
which sided with the faculty members at risk, questioned
Partridge's own academic background. Partridge challenged
faculty members with weak or no graduate credentials.
Others pointed out that Partridge's doctorate had been
earned at the Blackstone School of Law in Chicago through
correspondence courses. The attacks became vicious. The
complainants asked the Canadian Association of University
Teachers to intervene. When it did, it quickly became critical
of Partridge's handling of the cases. It proposed comprom-
ise solutions, which Partridge promptly rejected. The CAUT
Executive unanimously voted to censure UVic, a decision
that embarrassed and further aroused many on the UVic
campus.

Subsequently, a student petition and a faculty vote
declared their lack of confidence in Partridge. On 19 March
1971, in the wake of a "teach-in" on the issues, some sixty
students invaded his office. The CAUT Council then passed a

left | Bruce Partridge, president, 1969–72, pictured here at his
installation, 1969.

right | Students hold sit-in in President Partridge's office, 1971.

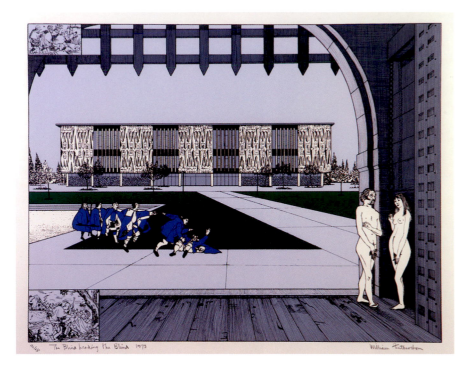

A copy of a silkscreen by William Featherston from the Faculty of Fine Arts, one of the people particularly affected by the turmoil of the early 1970s. He prepared the above as his comment on the situation; his way of showing the disruption that occurred – access to the library in the background, standing for the absorption of knowledge, was blocked (at least for some) by the machinations and disorder associated with the struggles within the administration. William Featherston was very disillusioned about UVic when he left but continued his remarkable career, becoming well-known and accomplished as an energetic and thought-provoking artist (see http://williamfeatherston.com/). The work hangs prominently in the Philosophy Department, many of whose members were particularly concerned about the problems of the early 1970s.

highly unusual motion censuring Partridge personally. It was the denouement of a tragedy.

Despite the increasingly untenable nature of his position, Partridge remained as president for a year afterward. It was an immensely difficult time for him as it was for the faculty members directly involved; they would all be forced to go through significant career changes, with all that meant for them and those depending on them. The CAUT censure lasted until 1975 and affected the university's capacity to attract outstanding faculty. The divisions among the faculty remained. Though the bulk of opinion on campus seems to have supported the faculty members in the dispute, a sizable group supported Partridge. Memories lingered for years and a strong "opposition mentality" emerged among some faculty members. "The campus shifted from being joyful and malleable."[11]

On the other hand, it is easy to dwell overlong on these disputes. Classes met. Students graduated. Faculty members taught well and pursued important research. Beneath the storm, UVic continued largely as it had been developing. Though weak in its handling of personnel issues, the central administration had developed some remarkable strengths. The coterie of devoted staff members carried over from the college days had been supplemented by individuals destined to play very important roles in the future development of UVic. Robert McQueen, from UBC, joined the university in 1962 as UVic's chief accountant and teacher of accountancy. A quiet, thoughtful person, with a deep commitment to UVic's teaching mission, he was a resourceful and adept administrator, a main reason why the university would avoid financial crises over the next thirty years when he served as the university's chief financial officer. In 1963, Dean Halliwell became chief librarian. He would hold that post until 1988, managing in his unique way one of the fastest-growing library systems in the Canadian university system. Trevor Matthews came from UBC in 1965 as an administrative assistant to the president. He quickly became responsible for the administrative side of the university, an immense challenge as the university grew. An ebullient, optimistic, determined, and forceful individual, he would have a remarkable impact on the campus over the following thirty years.

If you seek his monument, simply look around you when walking about the campus: he carefully oversaw its development, while also retaining high morale among the many non-faculty staff working at UVic.

The underlying growing strength of the administrative staff and the gathering determination of the bulk of the faculty to create a better UVic meant that "the year of troubles" was an incident, not a trend. In 1972, Hugh E. Farquhar became president (pro tem). A former mathematics teacher in the college, he was summoned, like Hickman and Wallace in other difficult times, to calm the turmoil. His normally calm demeanour helped reduce tensions; his preference for looking to the future, rather than dwelling on the past, helped change attitudes. Under him, the McPherson Library expanded, a new physical education complex was constructed, and long overdue reforms in appointment and tenure procedures were begun. In 1974, he presided over the opening of the Faculty of Law, destined to become very quickly one of Canada's best. In 1975, he received word that the CAUT would be lifting its censure of the university. UVic was back on course, not without wounds that still hurt, but ready for a great leap forward. It had survived the most "changin'" of times."

left to right | Robert J. McQueen, 1982; Dean Halliwell, 1977; Trevor Matthews, ca. 1965; Hugh E. Farquhar, president, 1972–74.

··· THE BUILDINGS OF 1963–1975: THE LEGACY ···

6

....

EXPANDING, 1975–1990

Howard Petch, president, 1975–90.

One day in late 1976, he strode into the vice-president's office and announced, a touch of elation in his voice, "George, I think we have turned the corner."[1] The speaker was Howard Petch. He had become president of the University of Victoria on 1 July 1975. The vice-president was George Pedersen.

Petch's roots lay in rural Ontario. He carried with him the rigorous determination, sense of duty, and flexible entrepreneurship that can be found in those roots – what some might call the positive attributes of Old Ontario. After military service, he had gone west to UBC, where he had gained a PhD in nuclear physics – and a "messianic zeal" for solid state/materials research and interdisciplinary programmes. He had become involved in federal government science policy, which provided him with a valuable overview of the multi-faceted development of scientific enquiry. That background would greatly influence his work at UVic, as would several years in administrative posts at McMaster and Waterloo universities. The time at Waterloo, one of Canada's most innovative universities, particularly shaped his views on the roles of universities in the modern world.

Before serious, sustained, and planned expansion could take place at UVic, however, the discordant inheritance of the previous few years had to be quieted. It happened, partly because of the constructive approaches of some emerging leaders within the faculty and in the Faculty Association: individuals such as I.D. Pal, Michael Ashwood-Smith, John Greene, Sam Scully, "Sandy" Kirk, Walter Young, and Richard Powers – faculty members who, in their different ways, were determined to reshape the university. They all went on to play very important roles within the university.

Ultimately, though, change relied mostly on the attitudes and efforts of several administrators, particularly Petch himself. Since many of the problems had been caused by a widening gulf between administrators and faculty members, his key objective was to create greater levels of trust. He spontaneously joined faculty groups for lunches in the Faculty Club. He introduced what became popularly called the "Petch procedures" – ratification votes for any candidates for administrative posts. All proposed administrators recommended by duly constituted search committees would have to be ratified in a secret ballot by 60 per cent of those they were being proposed to lead. Petch had advanced similar ideas at McMaster and Waterloo but had not been successful in getting them accepted. With the support of other

Aerial view of UVic ca. 1979.

administrators, the Faculty Association, and members of faculty, however, he was able to implement them at UVic.

Another innovation was a weekly open house (what became known as "Petch Peeves"), in which any university employee could bring complaints or concerns directly to him. Both steps, along with improvements in appointment, promotion, and tenuring procedures for faculty generally, helped reduce tensions considerably. They made possible a remarkable expansionist phase in UVic's history. It built upon growth begun during the Farquhar administration, most demonstrably identified with a Senate motion in 1973 authorizing the opening of "schools" serving professional groups. The only proviso was that they had to meet three criteria: have community support, be academically rigorous, and be financially viable.[2] This motion had opened the way for the schools that were added in 1975.

Petch's approach to expansion required increased long-term planning procedures, which were spearheaded by Jim Currie in an expanded administrative unit called Institutional Analysis. One of Currie's early projects showed that British Columbia relied heavily on attracting qualified professionals in engineering,[3] health services, business, and the law from other provinces, claims that UBC disputed. Currie's findings nevertheless became the basis for UVic's arguments for growth, as did a more basic appeal to helping "our own sons and daughters, nieces and nephews"[4] pursue their interests closer to home. Petch and others took the case out to communities around the province where it was well received, though perhaps less enthusiastically at UBC.

The most important dimensions of expansion, however, are not found in new programmes, more buildings, or even in increasing numbers of students and faculty. They lie in mentalité: how the people directly and indirectly involved view the new forms of learning being created; how well the universities relate to the communities that are being engaged. That was the significance of having "turned the corner." What Petch had perceived was the beginnings of significant support, not universal but strong enough, for expansion and new initiatives. The subsequent expansion took place on three levels – the broadening of curriculum, the deepening of new ways of knowing, and the gradual reconfiguration of the university.

....

BROADENING

The most obvious and publicized form of growth – the broadening of research and teaching activities – was seen in several new programmes. They would help transform what had been a limited four-year degree granting college into a much more diversified institution with expanded undergraduate offerings, more graduate programmes, and deepened research activities. They would provide a plethora of new ways of knowing, involving new subject matters, different methodologies, and (in many instances) expanded relationships with outside communities.

Many of them, in fact, were responses to specific social and economic issues. Despite their apparent affluence, the Greater Victoria area and British Columbia have always confronted unacceptably high levels of poverty, health problems, and social unrest. Three of the first schools developed by the university, therefore, were the Schools of Child Care (later Child and Youth Care), Social Welfare (later Social Work), and Nursing.

The programme in child care, which started formally in 1973, expanded as rapidly as it could, given the low number of practicum placements available for its students. It was an important initiative because of the plight of many young people in BC affected by fluctuating economies and uncertain income levels, extreme relentless poverty (often in remote places), any special needs they might have, and the impact of drugs on family life. UVic's child care programme was an important response to these challenges, a declaration of what should have been obvious; ensuring that the very young have a good start in life is a mark of a society's basic civility – it is also cheaper than dealing with adults stunted by a limited or abusive childhood.

Similarly, the development of social welfare was grounded in deep community problems, some essentially family issues writ large, others associated with basic patterns in BC life. For example, since the later nineteenth century, large transient populations have flowed through British Columbia and Victoria – youth seeking employment, families needing economic stability, immigrants adapting to Canadian life, seniors tired of snow, and First Nations people moving to cities. The social service system developed from the 1930s onward – generally civil society and parts of the Canadian welfare state – was hard-pressed to respond to these pressures, as it was to others emanating from rapid urban expansion, rural decline, and northern development.

At the same time, the province was coping with various major health issues. UVic responded by creating the School of Nursing in 1975. It was part of a general Canadian trend to replace hospital-based schools of nursing, the kind of nurse training institution that, everywhere except Quebec, had dominated the field since the late nineteenth century. Those institutions had understandably become primarily concerned with the immediate issues confronting their hosting hospitals rather than with detached professional development. The UVic School of Nursing, like those at other universities, wanted to include several university disciplines, new research, the systematic analysis of nursing, and (for many) the development of the nursing profession in their training.

The most contentious immediate issue at UVic proved to be over a more mundane matter than professionalization – money. The province originally had encouraged the School of Nursing's formation in the early seventies but, by the time it was ready to be developed, a government change had taken place and the new government was not as enthusiastic. It suggested that UVic find the funds from within its existing budget. Petch angrily refused.[5]

The stalemate was resolved when nurses all over the province, on their own initiative, organized a strong, vocal, and aggressive lobby, including twenty-eight nurses who had been involved with the programme as it had so far developed.[6] They were determined to have a programme solidly based on research involving several disciplines. They also knew about the needs in local communities better than anyone else. They phoned the Ministry of Education so often, it is alleged, that its telephone lines went down. A besieged minister, Pat McGeer, and a rather astonished government relented. The funds were found.

The fact the nurses involved in the campaign came from many parts of the province helped shape the school as it developed. The school started with a strong commitment to serving the needs of the provincial interior as well as Vancouver Island. It reinforced the strong commitment of the Education Faculty to the BC Interior. This emphasis was a part of a systematic effort at UVic, starting in 1977, to reach out more systematically to schools through-out the province, especially through gatherings of high school and college councillors invited to UVic for daylong workshops.[7] They came from many parts of the province, but particularly from the Okanagan and the Kootenays. UVic's debt to them and, more generally, to the smaller cities, towns and countryside beyond the larger urban centres of BC, is immense. It was not accumulated by accident.

This increased engagement with communities through concentrations on child care, social work, and nursing encouraged the university to reflect on relationships with the provincial government and to consider the formation of a full programme in public administration. It was not a new idea (Victoria College had offered a certificate for public servants) so it was not surprising that the university formed the School of Public Administration in 1974.

Under the leadership of it first two directors, Neil Perry and Rod Dobell, the school pursued a non-partisan approach to the public service (not easy in the political culture of British Columbia). It taught students multi-disciplinary, analytical skills so they would be able to provide the political leadership with sound, independent advice on public questions. In a world where short-term political needs tended to dominate, regardless of who is in office, this long-held ideal of public service was never more important – or more difficult to sustain.

left | Murray Fraser, dean of Law (1974–80), and vice-president academic (1983–88).

right | Howard Petch (left) and Murray Fraser (right) breaking the sod for the Begbie Building, as the Law Faculty's building was first called.

In 1977, the Schools of Nursing and Social Work and the Programme in Child Care (it became a school in 1979) formed a new faculty – Human and Social Development. Shortly afterward, the School of Public Administration, which taught only at the graduate level, joined the faculty, a unique blending of interests within the Canadian university system.

The Faculty of Law, created in 1974 with strong support from lawyers in the Victoria area, was another major addition. The first dean, Murray Fraser, came from Dalhousie University in Halifax. He brought with him the Dalhousie Law Faculty's strong commitment to teaching about law in society as well as about the technical side of the law. The faculty's programme, for example, began with a programme in legal process, "a philosophical approach to legal studies and law as social policy."[8] This approach fitted in well in the Victoria community and with UVic's Liberal Arts tradition. It also meant that an extensive and broad legal library was necessary, a task carried out enthusiastically by Diana Priestley. Judged by her colleagues the "best law librarian in Canada," she turned down a senior position in the library of the Supreme Court of Canada in order to come to UVic.[9] Within a year, she had secured 35,000 volumes for the library, which was located in a handsome new building, originally named for Matthew Begbie, the first chief justice of the Crown Colony of British Columbia. Over the next few years, Priestley, thanks largely to a donation of $600,000 from the Law Society of British Columbia, built up a substantial collection. Her grateful colleagues named the library after her.

Next came the Engineering Faculty. In one way the timing for this addition was propitious. The traditional engineering world – electrical, mining, civil, and mechanical – was being transformed by computing. A new faculty would be able to absorb this development easier than an old one and doing so would permit it to have a dramatic impact on the rest of the campus.[10] UVic attracted Professor Len Bruton, a prominent computing specialist from the University of Calgary, to help develop the idea. He was a particularly appropriate choice for UVic because he was also committed to developing a curriculum that would encourage engineers to consider the social impact of their work and to explore how they could work effectively with other professionals and communities.

The proposal to form the new faculty, though, was controversial. UBC was not supportive. Some UVic scientists feared that "applied science" would drain resources from "pure science." Existing programmes, for example the Applied Physics programme in the Physics Department, could be adversely affected. Others, notably in the humanities, were concerned that another professional school would further undermine what remained of the Liberal Arts tradition. Some were opposed to the further physical development of the campus. Jeremy Tatum, from the Physics Department, addressed those concerns in one of the most memorable speeches ever given at a meeting of the Faculty of Arts and Science. After playing a rhapsodic recording of skylarks singing, he claimed that such songs would be lost should further development continue. It was a poignant speech on behalf of those who regretted the university's rapid growth, the loss of the small and familiar, and the destruction of UVic's natural surroundings. Despite his eloquence – and that of the birds – the university ultimately approved the formation of the new faculty.

The proposal was submitted to the BC government in 1982, and shortly afterward, the premier of the day, Bill Bennett, announced his government's support for it. Bruton was appointed its first dean and students were admitted through the Faculty of Science for the academic year 1982–83.

When UVic first opened skylarks were commonly seen. Those who loved birds missed them as they gradually moved away.

Unfortunately, just at that time the provincial economy slowed, leading to severe government budget cuts. The creation of the faculty also became entwined with an election in May 1983 in which the future of universities became an important issue. Several UVic faculty members, mostly in the Departments of Political Science and Sociology, became very involved in the ensuing debates, mostly criticizing the Bennett government.[11] Government funding for the faculty was delayed.

As tensions developed, the government suggested that UVic close down some social science departments as a way to fund the faculty. President Petch and the board resolutely refused to do so. Petch, in fact, in a public, well-attended faculty meeting indicated that he would rather close the Engineering Faculty. Amid the uncertainties, Bruton returned to the University of Calgary. The attendant publicity finally triggered support from the government. The physicist John Dewey, who played many valuable roles at UVic during the 1970s and 1980s, took over briefly after Bruton left. Shortly afterward, a new dean, Eric Manning, arrived from the University of Waterloo.

The faculty moved forward quickly, developing programmes initially in electrical and computing engineering. Manning became "a change agent" within UVic, lobbying aggressively for longer hours for the library, an improved computing system, aggressive fundraising, more rigorous employment practices, increased student recruiting efforts, and more demanding search committees for university appointments. He promoted the co-op education programme like the one he had known at the University of Waterloo.

The Engineering Faculty, with some success, consciously sought to develop a "comfortable place" for women and minorities. Many university engineering programmes in North America did not have that reputation. It also sought to inculcate a team approach to learning about engineering through various special projects.[12] It even encouraged loyalties to the "Brotherhood of Engineers" – a concept that (despite its name) transcended masculinity and re-emphasized engineering traditions going back to the nineteenth century.

During the 1980s, discussions also began about starting a business faculty, though not everyone welcomed the idea. Some faculty members, notably those within the Liberal Arts tradition, opposed its development, fearing it would be too expensive and would become a programme in "training" not in education (as they interpreted the word). On the other hand, it was hard to deny that the province needed more trained business people than could be provided by UBC and Simon Fraser University. The Victoria business community, as represented by newspaper entrepreneur David Black and the Victoria Chamber of Commerce, vigorously agreed. The result was an intense discussion over some two years that successfully steered amid the shoals of community, government, and campus interests. At the end, it produced a particularly thoughtful and balanced report, one that led to the creation of the Business School.

These efforts to create new faculties were the most obvious ways in which the university expanded. They can be seen as extensions of the social concerns of the 1960s. Some of them, especially those addressing social issues, flowed directly from the activism of the 1960s. Others demonstrated the connection through their social concerns, their associations with communities, and with the social consequences of what they did.

The inheritance of the 1960s, though, was most evident in UVic's engagement with gender issues and environmentalism. Both were open-ended in their commitments; neither could be conveniently bottled up. Both challenged the university in very fundamental ways: in what was taught; in how it was taught; in how the university was structured; and in how the future should be planned. Perhaps most importantly, they challenged the society of which the university was a part.

Like most Canadian universities, UVic in the 1970s seemed to be (and in many ways was) largely a "man's world." Administrators were invariably male, as were the majority of the students (except in the Faculty of Education). Only fifty-two of the 417 regular faculty teaching at UVic in 1977–78 were women.[13] Within disciplines, the multiple roles of women in society tended to be ignored, even those that hardly had an excuse: for example, history, sociology, anthropology, English, cultural studies, and literature. Feminist thought typically received little attention in the areas of philosophy, political science, and economics, where it increasingly had much to say.

In 1975, a group of women undergraduates formed a UVic Women's Action Group to demand some feminist changes on campus. They asked for the further development of on-campus daycare, a Women's Centre, and courses in women's studies, courses like those being developed elsewhere in the country.[14] They approached Constance Rooke of the English Department, who recruited two other professors eager to help, Jennifer Waelti-Walters in French, and Paddy Tsurumi

The United Nations declared 1975 to be International Women's Year. It had a major impact on the treatment of women around the world. In Victoria, women's groups, including some from UVic, organized a march downtown. The march helped create a sense of urgency and purpose to the emerging gender issues on campus.

The three "founding mothers" of Women's Studies: left to right, Connie Rooke, Jennifer Waelti-Walters, and Paddy Tsurumi. Picture taken in 1989 during the celebration of the tenth anniversary of the establishment of Women's Studies. Photo courtesy of the Department of Women's Studies.

in History. The three of them, later joined by Phyllis Senese and Angus McLaren in History, started offering courses in 1979 focusing on women's history and women's literature. The School of Nursing developed a "caring curriculum" based on feminist theory and a belief in the special human qualities nurses bring to treating patients. Many in the community became enthusiastic. When Waelti-Walters began her first class in the Women in French Literature course, "all across the front row were ... elderly women ... and I said to myself, 'I can't give my lecture to these folk'... but I didn't have anything else. So I gave my lecture and all the good questions came from the front row. These women had been feminists for fifty years, waiting for a place to come out. It was amazing. And the (young) faces behind seemed to ask ... 'does my granny think like that?'"[15]

Others on campus soon joined the three founders: Marilyn Callahan (Social Work), Maureen Maloney (Law), Margie Mayfield (Education), Fong Woon (Pacific and Asian Studies), Phyllis Senese (History), Monika Langer (Philosophy), Hester Lessard (Law), and Brishkai Lund (Continuing Studies). Senior administrators, notably Howard Petch and Vice-President Academic Murray Fraser (1983–88), showed significant sympathy for the issues they were raising. Fraser, in fact, already alarmed by challenges confronting female law students, organized a consultative committee of about fifteen women faculty members drawn from across the campus. During 1986, he met with them regularly every Wednesday afternoon for several weeks in what became a challenging "learning" experience for him.[16] He was the only man in a room with fifteen to twenty determined, sometimes angry, women addressing complex, deep-seated issues about which they felt deeply, and for which, one way or another, he could be partly responsible. Sam Scully, his successor, did the same. As Waelti-Walters later recalled, "it was those meetings that really shifted things on campus."[17] From these meetings the Faculty Women's Caucus (latterly the Academic Women's Caucus) emerged, a group that over the next decade was remarkably successful in getting women's and feminist issues on the university agenda.

In 1983 an ad hoc women's studies committee drawn from faculties across campus hired Christine St Peter to develop the first interdisciplinary courses in women's studies. It was

for senior students and it proved to be instantly popular, despite its reputation as being too demanding. In 1987, the university launched a minor programme in the field and appointed her as the first tenure-track professor in Women's Studies, one of the first in the developing field in Canada. The programme developed steadily. Brishkai Lund helped fund some of the courses, but the primary support came from Vice-President Sam Scully (1988–96) who saw the programme into department status in 1995, and from the deans of Humanities (Edward Berry and Ian MacPherson) who gave the programme an institutional home.

Women's studies amounted to something of a paradigm shift in ways of knowing, breaking as it did from some of the traditional patterns of research and teaching. It did not conform comfortably to the ways in which research and teaching are typically pursued within universities – by building incrementally on established knowledge using what are believed to be impartial methodologies. It started from different assumptions, asked alternative questions, was particularly concerned with biases, and could be open to alternative solutions. It contrasted sharply with the common methods of sci-

left | Norma Mickelson, student of Victoria College, elementary school teacher, expert on reading, first female academic dean at a major Canadian university (Education, UVic, 1975–80), first UVic advisor to the president on equity issues (1986–91), first female president of the UVic Faculty Association (1989–90), and UVic chancellor (1996–2003).

right | On 6 December 1989, an enraged gunman wandered through the halls of Montreal's École Polytechnique and randomly killed fourteen women. The tragedy deeply affected many people at UVic, especially women. Each year people gather to mark the anniversary of the killings and to reflect on violence against women.

Environmental Studies became a very popular option for students during the 1980s. The poster below partly suggests why.

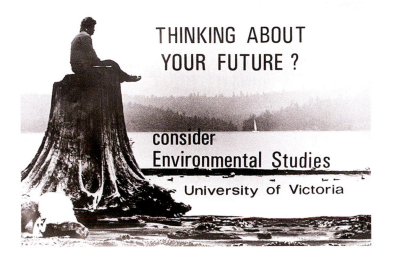

ence and, indeed, much social science. It was hardly surprising that its ways of knowing were not immediately appreciated in all corners of the campus.

The development of Women's Studies also took place amid growing concerns that any harassment of students, particularly women, be quickly and appropriately addressed. Petch asked Barbara Whittington (Social Work) to develop policies and educational programmes to address any problems. With the help of others, she developed the Human Rights Office in 1985, one of the first at any Canadian university. She helped found a national organization, the Canadian Association for the Prevention of Discrimination and Harassment in Higher Education, which continues to function, meeting the needs of universities in this important dimension of how they operate. She also assisted in the development of the Equity Office shortly thereafter. Human rights, equity, and harassment issues were being addressed at UVic; though, as at all universities, the issues, and the necessary education to deal with them effectively, would be a matter of years and considerable sustained effort.

Environmental studies also represented a significant and controversial paradigm shift, though in some ways, it seemed to fit in more easily at UVic. The central importance of the natural landscape had been apparent since UVic's first development plan appeared in the 1960s. A faculty outburst had stopped one proposal from that plan – to have magnolia trees line the main central courtyard. The faculty demanded indigenous, "natural" trees. During the 1960s and 1970s, too, UVic's development of flower gardens and natural spaces was widely applauded. In 1974, Mrs Jeanne Buchanan Simpson of Cowichan Lake willed a large collection of rhododendrons to UVic, and the idea of developing special gardens for them – the Finnerty Gardens – was widely supported. Concern for the natural environment had become ingrained in the vision of UVic held by many people on campus and in the community.

The development of the field of environmental science, of course, involved far more than the campus preferences for natural surroundings. By the 1970s, many faculty members and students were seriously engaging environmental issues, such as those raised by Rachel Carson in her remarkable book, *Silent Spring*.[18] Throughout BC, where the interplay between science and public policy was evident, UVic faculty members were encountering increased environmental concerns as they carried out their research and developed co-operative programmes. Environmentalism was becoming one of the pervasive issues of the age. As Alan Drengson of UVic's Philosophy Department recalls, "Public concerns about environmental problems began to grow in the mid '60s. This led to the first Earth Day in 1970 as people all over the world were eager to support corrective actions. There were deep appraisals of the industrial approach to primary production and energy use.

In North America the focused public concern gave rise to the grass roots environmental movement."[19]

UVic's awareness of environmental issues also reflected an awakening academic interest in the field of environmental studies. In 1972, Marc Bell (Biology) and Derrick Sewell (Geography), along with some other faculty members proposed the establishment of an Environmental Studies programme at UVic. Their proposal was viewed positively but cautiously and it was started in 1974, with a spartan budget of $2,500, no assigned space, and no specially assigned faculty.[20] It relied on the volunteer efforts of many faculty members and students drawn from across the campus – a not uncommon way in which new programmes were (and are) started at UVic. It became a regular programme in 1979 and soon several UVic researchers were researching environmental issues. Drengson recalls the discussions associated with the development of Environmental Studies:

> During the early years some thought that environmental problems could be solved mostly by technical means through science and technology. We can modify our systems, but not change our basic values and attitudes toward the Earth. Others, in the Social Sciences, for example in Economics and Political Science, thought that economic and policy matters should be the main focus. Some in the Humanities thought these problems involve our ultimate values and personal philosophies in conflict with the values of the ecosphere. Clearly, all aspects of the problems needed to be addressed. It was difficult then to say which should have priority.[21]

This kind of complexity meant that the advocates had to defend themselves against charges that they were not doing "real science" or were too preoccupied with transitory issues. The complexity, though, also whetted the interest of many beyond the science and geography departments to focus on environmental issues, including people in education, philosophy, and history. The Faculty of Law became particularly interested, and, in time, would create a chair in the field.

The Brundtland report on the environment, *Our Common Future*, commissioned by the United Nations and published in 1987, helped the environmental cause considerably. Its call for "sustainable development," the importance of meeting the needs of the world's poor, and for setting limits on what the wealthy should consume were important messages for the times. They helped people at UVic make the case for the growing and vital importance of environmental studies.

In 1987, Paul West, whose interest in environmental issues had grown while serving on several government organizations and while helping

Paul West, who contributed much to understanding environmental issues at UVic and served as director of the Environmental Studies programme, 1987–2001.

develop chemistry's co-op educational programme, became chair of the programme. He would serve for some twelve years. Passionate and energetic, determined and persistent, he made a major contribution in establishing the School of Environmental Studies at UVic. The first faculty member was appointed to the school in 1989, when the school joined the Faculty of Social Science. It grew steadily thereafter, attracting many students, expanding its faculty complement, and becoming increasingly more evident in the wider community.

During the 1980s another new initiative, the programme in Medieval Studies, emerged, developed mostly by faculty members in the Humanities Faculty. They recognized that the study of the medieval period required interdisciplinary approaches. The programme was launched in 1987 by John Tucker and Kathryn Kerby-Fulton from the English Department, Greg Andrachuk and Lloyd Howard from Hispanic and Italian Studies, and John Osborne in History in Art. They were strongly supported by the dean of Humanities at the time, Sam Scully. It began by offering a minor in medieval studies but in time would grow to include both major and honours programmes.

The fascination with the medieval era has been quietly important at UVic. As John Tucker puts it, "it's something that catches student interest – it's a world they would like to re-enter … [It provides] ways of imaginatively recreating a richer life … perhaps through values of heroism or aesthetic qualities."[22] The programme was also helped by a considerable interest in matters medieval within the community, an interest that was sustained by the Society for Creative Anachronism in Victoria in what they call the Kingdom of Tir Righ.[23] They – and many others in the community – have enthusiastically supported the Medieval Studies' annual workshop, which began in 1988. Each year, it has brought together 200 to 250 people to sample the wares of costumed medieval hawkers and to listen to papers, many of them delivered by leading medieval scholars from Europe and North America. They explore topics such as animals in the medieval world, medieval Jerusalem, the search for King Arthur, medieval law, and love (both sacred and profane). In a world where the present is too much with us, it provides a window into another world, strikingly different yet eerily the same as our own; one that can still cause people to pause and wonder.

Such developments do not happen easily. New initiatives typically must compete vigorously for acceptance and resources, including those pushed by existing departments. Before much can be added, something valued must sometimes be left behind, occasionally including what some faculty members, students, and others have devoted their lives to developing. Life's transience is nowhere more apparent than in university curricula. What was yesterday's brilliant article or book becomes today's straw man.

The Medieval Fair became a lively and colourful annual event at UVic during the 1980s. It still is, as this photo from 2011 demonstrates.

DEEPENING

Fascinations with the new (or apparently new) should not detract from the valuable understandings built up carefully and incrementally over generations. The older disciplines, the older ways of knowing, usually expand in undramatic ways, but their expansion is central to any university's development. Their methods, developed over decades of earnest efforts, do not suddenly become obsolete despite the siren call of the latest innovation – or fad. The established disciplines constantly evolve as new methodologies appear, as scholars change approaches, and as new interests emerge. "Old" topics still supply new insights and knowledge. The last word has not yet been written on Shakespeare, Montaigne, and Dante. New media reinterpret cultures and old stories. The unending and cumulative findings of "traditional" science still transform our age.

The growth and the deepening of scientific enquiry at UVic became a powerful force between 1975 and 1990. The science departments were arguably in the forefront in expanding research activities, in changing how decisions on annual salary recommendations, promotion, and tenure were made,

left | Fred Fischer, chemist, dean of Arts and Science (1975–78 and 1978–79), vice-president academic (1978–83), and academic leader in many other roles.

centre and right | In the early 1970s few appreciated how deadly and common was hypothermia. Few had explored how to deal with it effectively. John Hayward, a thermal biologist, worked with a friend, John Erickson, and Martin Collis, from UVic Physical Education, to explore survival rates in cold water, the effect of age and weight, and the effectiveness of different kinds of protective gear. Their research led to the development of Mustang jackets, now made in Vancouver and distributed throughout North America, a common sight wherever there is cold weather. In the centre photograph, Hayward wears one of the jackets. The other picture shows his work with a student on exploring the impact of cold water.

The Chemistry Department, 1980, one of the most influential and important departments at UVic.

and in attracting graduate students. The science departments made numerous outstanding appointments in that period and all the science departments – Chemistry, Biochemistry, Physics and Astronomy, Biology, Microbiology, and Mathematics – flourished. Each possessed strong champions on campus and several science faculty members profoundly influenced the university during the 1970s and 1980s. Fred Fischer, a New Zealand chemist, for example, was instrumental in helping build his department and faculty. As vice-president academic (1978–83) he helped guide UVic through an exciting and often very challenging period of growth. A steady, rigorous, and frank leader, he made a major contribution to the university throughout his long career. Others, such as Alex McAuley, Reg Mitchell, Graham Branton, and Paul West (also from Chemistry), Bill Gordon and Roger Davidson (Mathematics), Al Matheson (Biochemistry), and John Weaver (Physics), for example, all played important roles in articulating and promoting the roles of science on campus and in the community.

The expansion of the science departments severely strained the university's capacity to provide them with space, resources, and research support. In the later 1960s, new appointments could have only small sections of a bench and some $600 to spend on their own research. The senior professors possessed only small personal, rather than substantial, research laboratories. That situation changed significantly during the mid-1970s, partly because of the demands of recent appointments, partly because of increased research funding. In 1978, the federal government established the Natural Sciences and Engineering Research Council (NSERC). Possessing more resources than its predecessor, the National Research Council, it transformed scientific research at Canadian universities over the following two decades. It encouraged larger, more substantial projects, often involving groups of scientists and employing substantial numbers of graduate students.

UVic scientists responded very effectively to this shift, though it was not easy during much of the 1980s when budgets were very tight at UVic.[24] Their capacity to produce increasingly important research results expanded as the decade wore on. They were engaged with international science activities and networks. Their research "measured up" well against international competition as indicated by research contributions, dollars attracted, and recognition (for example, through citations in scientific and other journals).

Several successes were particularly noteworthy. The Chemistry Department, for example, developed to become one of the strongest departments on campus (some of its foremost admirers, not least in the department itself, thought of it as *the* strongest). In Biology, George Mackie, who would become one of UVic's most prominent international scholars, pioneered in some of the university's most important early work on the Pacific Ocean, in his case especially on the less well-known animals that lived there. The Department of Biochemistry and Microbiology became one of the most successful departments in Canada measured by its successful applications to NSERC. Some members of the Physics Department continued to practice what they called "suitcase physics," travelling regularly to other universities to carry out some of their work. A common destination was UBC where they continued their remarkable work with Canada's

left | The observatory on top of the Elliott Building, used by generations of students in the university's popular astronomy programme, part of the Department of Physics and Astronomy. Three students, allegedly leaving "the library" late one evening, somehow managed to skirt security and painted the smile face over twenty years ago, and it has survived. The astronomer Colin Scarfe is standing in front of the observatory.

right | Students on a field trip to Bamfield in 1977.

National Laboratory for Particle and Nuclear Physics located on its campus. Several UVic scientists, notably Lyle Robertson and George Beer, were playing a particularly important role in its development by the mid-1970s. Others travelled regularly to the CERN Laboratory in Geneva, Switzerland, one of the world's most important physics laboratories, to carry out their work in atomic physics. Others in astronomy took advantage of the national observatory in nearby Saanich as well as observatories in Hawaii and Peru to gain international recognition for their work – and to inspire generations of students. The astronomy instructors, in fact, gained a remarkable reputation among students as teachers for the efforts.

The Biology Department garnered impressive international reputations in forest biology and microbiology. In 1972, it joined with other universities to form the Western Canadian Universities Marine Biological Society, which purchased facilities in Bamfield (on the west coast of Vancouver Island) constructed in 1926 as the starting point for the Trans-Pacific Cable. As the 1970s progressed, the facility was converted into a marine research station, particularly for marine biology. It developed teaching facilities and was soon welcoming each year over 100 students to its summer courses. It became a bustling yearlong research facility for faculty and students from both British Columbia and Alberta.

Bamfield signalled a deepening UVic interest in the oceans and not only in biology. When the Physics Department was asked, along with other departments, to define its future interests in the later 1980s, it decided, after much thought, that one of them was ocean physics. The department successfully made its case and soon after appointed Chris Barnes from the Geological Survey of Canada, one of Canada's most important researchers in the field, to develop ocean studies at UVic. His appointment helped spark interest in several other departments. Ocean studies would grow to become one of the university's most important initiatives.

Across the campus, similar signs of eager and effective innovation were evident. In Education, for example, largely through the efforts of Ted Owen, the university developed important relationships with China. It negotiated a formal connection (that is, one formally approved by governments) with a Chinese university – East China Normal University in Shanghai. UVic was the first North American university to sign such an agreement, stimulating several exchanges, including a very popular summer school for UVic students in Shanghai.

Other parts of the campus also showed a growing interest in Asia. In 1987, the university created the Centre for Asia-Pacific Initiatives (CAPI) to co-ordinate and facilitate that widening interest, notably in China, Japan, Southeast Asia, Korea, and the developing island states of the Southwest Pacific. In collaboration with the Department of Pacific and Asian Studies

East China Normal University students studying at UVic, hosted at a luncheon by President Howard Petch, 1986.

in the Faculty of Humanities (where most of the teaching about the region occurred), it significantly increased university engagement with the rich diversities and rapid development of parts of the immense Asia/Pacific region. More Asian students became evident on campus, notably in computing, mathematics, and some of the sciences, though they accounted for less than 2 per cent of the total student population. The doors to the East had been opened.

Throughout the period, as these interests developed, the university tried to attract more and more prominent scholars. One of the ways it did so was to use what became known as the Lansdowne Fund for that purpose. It was

In 1981, UVic held a special convocation in China to confer an honorary degree on Soong Ching Ling, widow of Sun Yat Sen. She had been an influential person in China for nearly fifty years and a leader in improving conditions for children.

a fund built up through the sale of lands that had been accumulated during the college years. The fund was used for two purposes. One was to appoint a sprinkling of Lansdowne chairs across the university, senior appointments that brought thriving research activities and very useful expertise to the university. The second use was to sponsor visits by "people of absolutely outstanding stature,"[25] distinguished researchers, to several departments each year, important events for students and the community as well as faculty. All told, the Lansdowne programme made a remarkable contribution to campus life, bringing some of the best scholarship in the world to UVic and raising issues on campus and in the community for discussion.

Despite the financial pressures and the debates over expansion, the faculties of UVic generally made substantial progress during the Petch years. They often were able to make appointments to replace retiring faculty members or to staff new projects. Since the period was characterized by a decline in hirings at most other universities, UVic was able to make several outstanding appointments, mostly at the junior level, meaning that within a decade it was developing outstanding research projects in many areas, and not just in the sciences. Some of these projects were:

- The Shakespeare Music Catalogue, undertaken by Bryan Gooch and David Thatcher from the English Department.
- The Vancouver Island Project, undertaken by Chad Gaffield and Peter Baskerville in the History Department, who worked with archivists to create a computerized research base for the Island's history.
- Fitness programmes for Canadian athletes in the America's Cup Race and the 1984 Olympics, developed by David Docherty and Howie Wenger.
- Computer assisted legal instruction on campus and with other law schools in Canada prepared by John Kilcoyne and his students in the Faculty of Law.
- A Native Education programme in Hazelton – the beginnings of a significant effort to revitalize and preserve Indigenous culture developed by the Faculty of Education, in collaboration with the Gitsan-Carrier Tribal Council.
- *Etait-il une fois?*, a bibliographic guide to French and French-Canadian children's literature, compiled by Danielle Thaler and colleagues in the French Department.
- The Public History Group organized by Eric Sager, Peter Baskerville, Ken Coates, and Ian MacPherson in the History Department.
- Studies by Martin Segger and Anthony Welch demonstrating that arts-related industries employed over 1,200 workers in Victoria and collectively had payrolls of over $13 million annually, leading to the development of arts councils and special projects in the Capital Regional District.
- Participation in five new Centres of Excellence at Canadian universities established in 1989: Molecular and Interfacial Dynamics; Bacterial Diseases; Microelectronic Devices, Circuits and Systems for Ultra-Large Scale Integration; Telecommunications Research; and Robotics and Intelligent Systems.

In 1983, Queen Elizabeth and Prince Philip visited Victoria. In this picture President Petch escorts Queen Elizabeth through a reception line at UVic.

The University Centre opened in 1978, providing a place for concerts and an impressive location for convocations. The inaugural concert, held on 27 September 1978, conducted by George Corwin, featured the university orchestra and the university choir.

RECONFIGURING

In 1975–77, just over 400 regular faculty members at UVic taught nearly 7,400 students. In 1989–90, 580 regular faculty members taught over 13,000 students.[26] The long-held (but never formally-adopted) wish to limit the size of the university to some 10,000 students was a memory; the earlier "cap" of 5,000, considered as ambitious by some in 1963, was a forgotten footnote. The growth was not achieved without some pain: the government grant to the university per full-time equivalent fell from just under $6,000 to under $4,000 in those years.[27] Despite the attendant problems, the desire to do more was irresistible. The natural entrepreneurial tendencies of administrators, faculty members, departments, faculties, and students – particularly graduate students – were unquenchable.

The expansion was partly physical. The gently separated buildings around a restful central core, evident since the mid-1960s, were augmented by several new buildings. The McKinnon sports complex was opened. The University

left | The opening of the Phoenix Theatre Building in 1981 meant the closure of the old theatre located in one of the old army barracks, Q Hut.

right | The opening of the University Centre meant that convocations became increasingly impressive ceremonies. This picture of the spring convocation of 1989 shows the procession being led by Nels Granewall (front right), who for many years was the marshal for the parade.

Live theatre became increasingly popular during the late 1970s and 1980s as the new theatres attracted larger audiences. The students on the left are promoting a summer play. The students on the right are actors in a 1987 production of *The Importance of Being Earnest* – for some reason it seemed particularly to appeal to Victorians.

Centre was completed. Three buildings were added to form an attractive fine arts complex on a southwest quadrant beyond the Ring Road. The Begbie Building was constructed, also outside the Ring Road, as were three new residences and a new faculty club. An Interfaith Chapel was added and a new science/engineering building was built. By 1990 UVic's built environment had been dramatically changed.

The new construction generally followed the original plan developed in the early 1960s. Trevor Matthews and his staff, along with Howard Petch and the planning committee that guided the university's development, deserve much of the credit for ensuring that the natural surroundings remained prominent. Plants and new trees were planted in abundance when construction ended. The grounds staff of the university was remarkably diligent in carefully maintaining what had become for many the university's defining characteristic. When the national meetings of academics – then called the Learned Societies – met at UVic in 1990, the most common comment made by the over 7,000 who came was about the "natural" environment of the campus. As several wrote, it made UVic a "special place."

Growth inevitably meant, however, that there were questionable differences in the student experience at UVic. It is the standard universal concern when universities grow larger. It is exacerbated, as it was at UVic in the mid-1980s, by declining funds and by growing student concerns about grades and the increasing competition to enter professional and graduate schools. The growing number of students invariably meant larger classes and less student/professor contact, particularly in the social sciences where enrolment pressures were very intense. UVic sought to deal with the challenges by reconfiguring classrooms to fit the large lecture and seminar formats that were increasingly the norm. In 1981, it opened the *Learning and Teaching Centre* in the Law Faculty. While some older faculty members questioned the expenditure involved, most did not: they realized that the old method of teaching swimming in rural areas – "throw them in and see how they do" – was hardly appropriate any more for the development of university teachers. In 1984, Andy Farquharson from the School of Social Work became the centre's director. For the next fifteen years he would build it to become an important part of the campus, encouraging excellence in teaching, training teaching assistants, and helping graduate students wanting to learn how to teach.

One response to the concerns over how student life was developing at UVic was to emphasize sports. When Petch first came to UVic, he stayed in the student residences for a few months and became particularly aware of student attitudes at the time. He became concerned because he thought he detected "a certain amount of alienation" among them, an observation confirmed by alumni and some students. "They thought somehow they were there, but that something was missing."[28] Petch worked with others to develop a more energetic and prominent athletics programme, both intramural and intercollegiate, partly as a way to enrich the student experience on campus. He also believed that a strong intercollegiate programme could attract community interest, including members of the media, people interested in watching outstanding athletes compete in a variety of sports.

It was not a difficult emphasis to develop. From the 1880s onward, Victorians had been noted for their interest in sports of various types, including golf, cricket, soccer, rugby, running, basketball, and tennis. Victoria College, in fact, had benefitted from those traditions. Despite its comparatively small size, it had been able to compete effectively with teams from the much larger UBC and sports clubs in Vancouver. That was partly why the weekend excursions to the mainland had been so enjoyable – winning always made for better parties. Moreover, while general interest in intercollegiate sports at UVic was then small, student engagement in athletic activity was high. As Petch recalls, "everybody – and the students in

Andy Farquharson (Social Work), the leader and inspiration for the early development of the Learning and Teaching Centre.

75

··· BUILDINGS, 1975–1990: THE LEGACY ···

residence – were all jogging or doing one thing or another – far more physically active than our students at Waterloo. This impressed me greatly."[29]

In the later 1970s, as financial pressures on the university increased, building a sports programme became difficult. The cost of participating in intercollegiate sports was becoming increasingly expensive, and there were limited outside funds to help out. The need to specialize, given Victoria's particular assets – its year-long outdoor training possibilities being perhaps the most obvious – pointed the way to what was reasonable. A task force chaired by Ian Stewart and Judge Robert Hutchison in 1978 recommended focusing on a relatively few sports that were associated with local strengths, traditions, and suitability. They chose basketball, rugby, soccer, and track and field – all sports with strong local support and for which UVic had facilities and expert coaching available. They did not recommend engagement in such sports as hockey and football, where participation costs would be very high.

The expansion in sports programmes gathered momentum in 1975 as the McKinnon sports complex was opened and Ken Shields was hired as coach for the men's basketball team, the Vikings (often called the Vikes – the same name as all other UVic teams, regardless of sport or gender). He was determined to develop a team that would be largely, if not entirely, drawn from Vancouver Island. It was the beginning of a men's basketball dynasty, soon followed by another in woman's basketball, coached by Cathy Shields. Within two years, as the successes mounted, Ken Shields had been promoted to athletic director.

Other successes were soon evident in rugby, rowing, and especially women's field hockey. UVic quickly became one of Canada's premier universities in intercollegiate athletic competition. In the later 1970s, UVic collaborated with the national and provincial rowing and middle distance running sports organizations to create national training centres, a step that helped bring outstanding coaches and athletes to the Victoria area. By the end of the decade, eleven national coaches were coaching at UVic. Their successes, "publicity you cannot buy," did much to help put UVic on the map.[30] They became reasons why many students wanted to come to the university.

Shields put his stamp on the athletic programme as it developed during the 1980s. His primary perspective was captured in the following words: "I believe that universities should be about excellence and that athletics should be a model of excellence for the community. If you say you are going to profess excellence then the product and the way you conduct yourself should reflect that value at the highest level. I didn't see any conflict in the university striving for national and international standards in academics and in striving for the same in athletics."[31]

··· ATHLETICS ···

1987 CANADIAN NATIONAL CHAMPIONS

By the early 1980s UVic was becoming known for its excellence in coaching in several sports, leading to a large contingent of UVic athletes, including Eli Pasquale (above), participating in the 1984 Olympics.

At the same time, students were provided with intramural and recreational sports. Their use of the athletic resources was protected. Welcoming chip trails were built in the woods that remained on one third of the campus. By the late 1980s, despite the growth in student numbers that put a strain on the university's recreational and fitness facilities, Petch's observations about the level of student involvement in physical activities were still valid. And thirty years later, they still ring true.

During the 1980s UVic began systematically to recruit more students in BC and other provinces. It particularly targeted students from the rural areas of the province, a natural focus growing out of the interests of the Normal School/Faculty of Education and the School of Nursing. It was also connected to the rural backgrounds of several people teaching at UVic, including Petch. Perhaps most fundamentally, this recruitment strategy emanated from the realization that many deserving and capable students in rural districts were not attending university for economic, cultural, and family reasons. They deserved better. The university therefore concentrated much of its recruitment activities on the province's interior. By the mid-1980s, students from rural areas were the second largest grouping of students at UVic.

The university also expanded its extension programme, which had begun modestly during the college era. In 1969, Larry Devlin, a former college student who had studied adult education at the University of Chicago, returned to UVic to assist Bob Wallace, then acting president and the founder of the college's Evening Division. The enrolments grew steadily thereafter and by the mid-1970s, the university was expanding its services within the city and beyond. It worked with faculties, notably Education and Human and Social Development (particularly Nursing), to develop very successful programmes around the province. One of its more notable innovations, begun in the early 1970s, was the Hazelton Project, a teacher preparation programme designed specifically for the Gitxsan and Wet'suwet'en peoples who lived in that community.

Extension (or Continuing Education, as it became known in 1970) was in the forefront of understanding and responding to community changes. It tended to embrace innovative teaching methods earlier than other parts of the university. It believed that, in addition to research and teaching, universities had a third function – service.[32] Devlin brought that idea from his graduate work at the University of Chicago, where he had learned about the extensive rural co-operative extension programmes in the United States with their commitments to "connect the knowledge of the university with the needs of human beings"[33] through the development of co-operative organizations.

The Division of Continuing Education expanded its non-degree programme considerably, organized French and other language programmes, co-ordinated departmental offerings so as to ensure appropriate variety, and developed certificate/diploma programmes. It organized classical music weekends, in which students stayed in the residences. The programme was virtually non-stop, and the stamina of the professors was remarkable. Most instructors in the Extension courses came from the faculty but some came from the community. At one time, Devlin proposed creating an Extension College as a way to make a clear commitment to the service responsibilities. Amid the plethora of new initiatives of the times, it did not gain sufficient support.

During the 1980s the Division played an increasing role in addressing pressing community issues. Brishkai Lund, for example, responsible for developing extension programmes in the humanities and social sciences, organized numerous workshops, short courses, and public events addressing major social issues of the day, such as poverty, feminism, ecology, and immigration throughout the eighties and the decade that followed. She was a key figure in defining the university's social conscience.

As has unfortunately been the case at most Canadian universities, the Division was always vulnerable whenever the university came under financial pressures.[34] It had few faculty appointments and physical facilities, undertook limited research, and had less permanent budget allocations – in fact, it was expected to create surplus revenues. It had few of the defences academic units possessed.

The age of the computer arrived at UVic during the 1970s and 1980s. It came originally in the form of the mainframe computer, a highly centralized system that operated as a service facility for nearly everyone on campus. It was a monolithic approach that served particularly well people with limited understanding of computers – which included nearly everyone on campus at the beginning. Rather quickly, certainly by the later 1980s, though, some faculty members and some units wanted more flexibility in developing their own computing services.[35] Faculty members with NSERC funding were purchasing computers for students and themselves and became less dependent upon the mainframe. The rapid

The heart of the UVic Computer Centre in the 1980s.

Frank Robinson, chemist and student advisor.

evolution of computing, one dimension of which was placing more power in the hands of individuals – and another of which was the constant desire (maybe need) to change both hardware and especially software frequently – had arrived. It would be a complex and non-stoppable determining force, loved by some, detested by others.

UVic, despite the pressures of the 1975–90 period, was a socially friendly place. Student life was generally laid-back, serious but leavened by a busy pub life, a welcoming and safe city, pleasant study places, an attractive natural environment, and good teachers. Frank Robinson from the Chemistry Department can stand as a symbol of their best efforts. One of the few people of African descent on campus, he had lived through the civil rights struggles in his native Georgia and could readily sympathize with students confronting difficulties. As associate dean for the Advising Centre in the Faculty of Arts and Science, he and his staff dealt with large numbers of students in a compassionate yet fair and rigorous way, complementing well the work of Student Services. For his efforts he was made an honorary alumnus of UVic, an appropriate recognition of his work.[36]

Within academic departments, though some were divided over methodological/ideological debates and rocked by gender issues, most were well-known for their general pleasantness and tolerance. Relations between the Faculty Association and the administration generally improved during the later 1980s, though demands persisted for a more formal and clearer relationship.

The non-faculty, numbering about 300 by the mid-1970s (400 by 1990), included many people who had worked at the university for decades. Social events for staff, such as picnics and seasonal parties, were common. The influence of the administrative leaders, notably Trevor Matthews, Bob McQueen, and Dean Halliwell, was pervasive, some would say paternalistic, but certainly reassuring for those who worked hard. Despite the challenges, UVic was a good place to be, whatever role one might play.

PROMOTING, 1990–2000

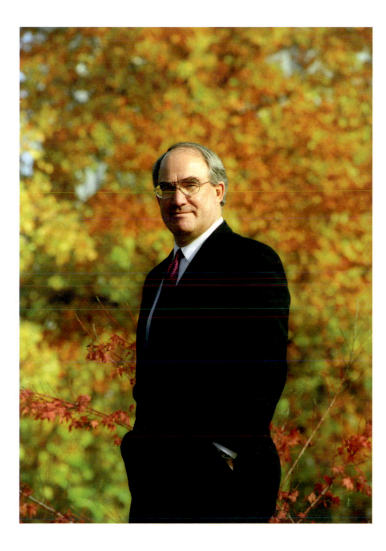

David Strong, president, 1990–2000.

David Strong's presidential installation process in October 1990 was unusual. Previously, UVic installations had generally been low-key affairs. This one, however, featured a special convocation, carefully planned to impress people on campus, in the community, and in the university world generally. There were two main reasons for the difference. Strong had a mandate from the Board of Governors, emphasized during the search process, to promote UVic aggressively so it would receive the recognition it deserved. The second was that he came from Memorial University of Newfoundland, which, despite its relative youth,[1] took ceremonies more seriously – perhaps because of closer ties with British universities. Strong brought that sense of occasion to UVic, and it would be a mark of his tenure.

The installation took place within a two-week "Installation Fest," which included music, theatre, exhibitions, lectures, sports, fireworks, and displays. Attracting 30,000 people to UVic,[2] it featured sessions on the environment, the challenges of an aging society, space and ocean issues, the nature of university presidencies, and the significance of academic traditions.

The ceremony itself had "pomp" in academic regalia, the installation rituals, and the granting of three special honorary degrees. It had "circumstance" provided largely by the university's impressive orchestra and choir, led by George Corwin. One piece they played was Handel's Coronation Anthem.[3] The ceremony lasted two hours, a rather emphatic way to underline its intended significance.

By the time the next convocation took place, Strong had implemented another Memorial practice by appointing university orators. The first orator was Sam Scully, the vice-president academic, followed by Juliana Saxton from Fine Arts and Anthony Jenkins from English. They were all skilled in one of the oldest academic disciplines, rhetoric, lamentably a declining art. Scully even delivered one of the orations in Latin, necessary when Prince Edward received an honorary degree in 1994. Many of the orations addressed issues beyond Victoria and British Columbia – a recurrent theme at UVic throughout the 1990s.

Strong was particularly enthusiastic about thinking internationally. A geologist by training, his work, starting on the "rock" of Newfoundland and Labrador, had taken him to the University of Edinburgh, long an international centre for studying geology. His PhD fieldwork was in the Comoro

Advertisement for the ceremony and associated activities of the installation of David Strong as president in October 1990.

Islands, off the east coast of Africa, where he concentrated on plate tectonics, the study of the large "plates" that shape life on our planet. Thereafter, from his Newfoundland base, he carried on similar research around the world. It was an exciting time for geology, a time when there was "a total explosion of new understanding of how the earth works,"[4] a time for a rereading of what rocks could reveal about the Earth's past. And it was international in scope – "if you are doing research in geology, you just have to go to where the rocks are. It makes you a traveller and gives you an appreciation of the rest of the world. If you wander through jungles and visit everywhere, when you come to a job like the president of a university you can't but have an international outlook."[5]

Strong's international enthusiasms fitted in well with contemporary preoccupations with the theme of globalization.[6] It particularly led him to concentrate on expanding UVic connections with Asia. In 1990, UVic joined the Co-op Japan Programme to help more UVic students find co-op work terms in Japan; it assumed administration of it a year later. It developed an Asia Partners Fund to fund research and exchanges; it had attracted $2 million by 2000.[7] It "internationalized" the curriculum, informally at first, more formally as the decade wore on.

International themes became more important in several departments. The History Department added world history to its undergraduate and graduate programmes. The Law Faculty deepened its interest in Asian legal systems, specifically Thailand, Indonesia, India, the South Pacific, and Vietnam, largely through the efforts of William Neilson and Jamie Cassels.[8] The Centre for Asia-Pacific Initiatives and the Department of Pacific and Asian Studies welcomed Asian scholars each year. They encouraged research on such topics as Thai social unrest, the treatment of Asian women, Asian shrimp farming, the economic history of the Pacific Islands, and several projects on China, including poetry, the effects of aging, revolutionary art, and trends among Chinese youth. The Faculty of Education expanded its successful work with the East China Normal University. Asian scholars and students came in greater numbers to UVic. UVic people journeyed across the Pacific: Neilson alone made over fifty trips to Vietnam between 1990 and 2010 to teach and do research.

The Asian impact on the UVic campus soon became more apparent through the work of the Division of Continuing Studies. Its directors, Michael Brooke (1992–97) and particularly Wes Koczka (1997–2007), and its staff developed one of Canada's most successful university second language programmes. It created the homestay programme so Asian students could board with local families. It welcomed groups of young Asian students, mostly from Japan and Korea, each year, especially during the spring and summer months.

Elsewhere, the Germanic Studies Department offered a very successful language/cultural programme in Kassel, Germany. Other language departments in time replicated its efforts. The Faculty of Business sent students overseas for work terms; other faculties followed suit. More faculty members, within and without the Department of Hispanic and Italian Studies, undertook research in Latin America. A few (arguably not enough) explored African themes, including orphan care in Malawi, African cinema, post-imperial African literature, and African childhood education. Others addressed Middle East subjects, such as Islamic art, Gaza settlements, the Arab-Israeli conflict, property rights, and war in the Persian Gulf. Ian MacPherson co-ordinated the process and wrote the documents whereby the International Co-operative Alliance, then representing 800 million members in local co-operatives worldwide, defined the nature, roles, and vision of the co-operative movement for the twenty-first century. UVic's windows on the world were opening wider.

As internationalism grew, UVic regularized its international work. In 1993–94 it developed policies regulating its international activities. By 1996, it had signed forty-five formal exchange agreements with universities outside Canada; by 1998, there were 111.[9] These exchange agreements governed student travel both ways, defined the kinds of academic credit that could be earned, and identified how faculty exchanges could be arranged.

Encouraged by these trends, Strong explored starting a centre devoted to global issues. He approached Gordon Smith, a federal public servant whose interest in international affairs was triggered during the 1962 Cuban Missile Crisis. It became the subject of his graduate work, leading to a career in the Department of External Affairs and a lifelong interest in peace issues. At various times, he served as deputy minister of Foreign Affairs, the prime minister's personal representative on the G7/G8 summits, and ambassador to NATO and the European Union. In 1997, he joined UVic to help start the Centre for Global Studies.

This global thrust was an exciting dimension of UVic during the 1990s. It altered teaching, encouraged different ways of knowing, influenced campus development, and engaged many faculty, students, and staff. It enlarged

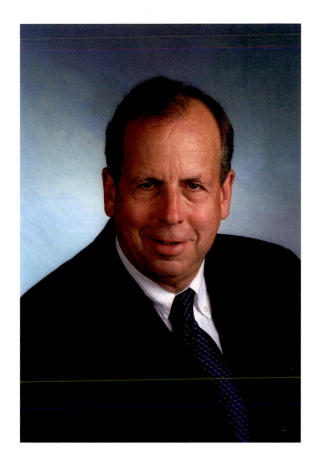

Gordon Smith, director of the Centre for Global Studies, 1988–2012.

Sam Scully, dean of Humanities (1983–87),
vice-president academic (1988–96).

connections with nearby immigrant communities. It helped demonstrate
that UVic, as in previous times, was not a place of somnolent introspec-
tion – an ivory tower above the fray.

....

TEACHING

As the globe shrank during the 1990s, the local situation loomed larger.
Between 1990 and 2000 student enrolments increased from 14,000 to
17,500. This growth tended to spread student loyalties thinly, making more
important relationships with friends in the programmes in which they were
enrolled. It is difficult for students (and faculty) to sustain broad institutional perspectives as organizations grow, diversify, and become more complex. UVic was living through the "massification" of the academy – rapid
growth, new professional faculties, and larger class sizes.[10]

The growth invariably intensified questions about teaching. In 1992,
the vice-president academic, Sam Scully, in partnership with the Faculty
Association, appointed a committee, chaired by Tom Cleary from the
English Department, to investigate teaching effectiveness at UVic. It recommended "holding the line" on class size, expanding teacher training,
updating classrooms, and making teaching more important in salary, promotion, and tenure decisions.[11] Subsequently, departments reassessed teaching programmes and several UVic faculty members wrote articles on teaching for *The Ring*, the official campus publication. It was an important issue
that stimulated much discussion – and would not die.

The teaching discussions coincided with a deteriorating financial situation. The financial restraint of the 1980s worsened after 1992 partly because
UVic accepted some 500 more students each year between 1995–96 and
1997–98 without increases in the government grants for them. It did so by
enlarging classes and by hiring more sessional instructors (the number of
regular faculty actually declined from 605 to 592 in those years).[12] Many
"sessionals" were youthful, "recently minted" PhDs, who brought much
enthusiasm and new knowledge to their work. Many of them, however, paid
a heavy price, spending precious years teaching too many (and too many
different) courses as they searched for permanent positions (at UVic and
elsewhere). Only a few achieved their dreams. It was a sad dimension of
Canadian academic life then and afterwards – at UVic and everywhere else.

The enrolment expansion of the decade was nevertheless a remarkable
accomplishment, most obviously for the administrators responsible
for UVic's financial management – the senior financial and administrative managers, Robert McQueen (1963–92), Don Rowlatt (1992–99), and
Jack Falk (1999–2006) – and those responsible for teaching – the vice-

presidents academic, Sam Scully (1988–96), and Penelope Codding (1996–2001), the faculty deans, and department/programme leaders. Equally, though, faculty members deserve recognition for their acceptance of increased responsibilities.

The teaching issue grew as class sizes increased, sessional instructors became more numerous, and too many first year students did not complete their first year.[13] The Learning and Teaching Centre became more active. Its seminars on teaching methods and for graduate students earned widespread support – even from some faculty members who had originally regarded it as an unnecessary "frill." Its increased stature was marked by the construction of a building for it, named after Harry Hickman, one of Victoria College's (and UVic's) most highly regarded teachers.

The opening of the centre coincided with changes in the ancient art of teaching. Each year more strange small cameras appeared on classroom ceilings, accompanied by rather bewildering equipment at the front of the room. Chalk use declined, blackboards were perpetually clean, professors' jackets no longer bore chalk smudges, the historic and honorable badge of the profession. Overhead transparencies, regarded as revolutionary by some in the 1980s, became quaint relics. The computer had arrived in the classroom. Many faculty embraced PowerPoint presentations. Students clamoured for copies of them. Some faculty agreed; others did not, fearing reduced attendance and believing that the discussions about the material were as important as what they contained. It was a superficial version of a deeper question: was education primarily the distribution of information easily digested for mastering some competency? In an age when sound bites were replacing wisdom, it was not just a classroom debate.

Even the lecture system, that hallowed form of university teaching, came into question. By the 1990s, the development of online courses at the Open University and at UVic itself sparked enthusiasm for new ways of learning. The questioning was evident "at the top": the Chancellor, William Gibson, a long-time UBC instructor and a key BC educational leader, joined the fray, arguing for alternative, high quality forms of instruction.[14] New knowledge was shaking the university world; so was how it was communicated.

Until the late 1980s, it was assumed that humanists only needed a library and (maybe) a tape recorder. Then new technology made possible a Computer Assisted Language Facility (or CALL facility), which offered students a variety of ways to learn languages. The cost of UVic's facility was $750,000 initially. At the insistence of Sam Scully (dean and the vice-president), Peter Liddell from Germanic Studies became its director.

87

The financial pressures on students during the 1990s became intense, as this picture of students lining up outside the Financial Aid Office in 1991 suggests.

STUDENT LIFE

Student life changed markedly as the century ended. The financial price of attending university rose steadily. More students attended part-time so they could earn money. Growing numbers of single parent students struggled to juggle home, university, and work responsibilities. Student loans grew larger. For more students (and parents) education became a cost-benefit issue. The idea of attending university for personal development and deepening reflection – even for celebrating youth – was fading. Competition for grades intensified as graduate admission requirements rose, particularly in professional faculties – in some instances, discouragingly so. Professors felt those pressures, encouraging grade inflation (rising average grades), a subject for many fiery Senate debates. The times, they were continuing to change. Youth was fleeting faster than even poets imagined.

As the student body expanded, pressures on facilities and student services grew. The Student Union Building expanded significantly in the early 1990s. The University of Victoria Students' Society (UVSS) – the students had changed the name from the Alma Mater Society in 1989 – struggled to meet students' needs. In 1989, it assumed management of the Student Union Building. By the end of the nineties it was overseeing several businesses – food facilities, a pub, a printing business, a copy centre, a travel agency, and other student support services. It sought to operate those businesses "differently," particularly by emphasizing recycling; it became something of a campus leader in that respect. The UVSS had also become a remarkable training ground for students as they came together to run businesses – probably not the reason for which most student politicians had originally sought office.

The UVSS was a force for student activism, much of it concerned (as in the 1980s) with rising tuition costs and housing shortages. It advocated greater student involvement in university governance, notably on Senate and the Board and in departments. It encouraged course unions and sponsored course evaluations. Through *The Martlet*, the UVSS encouraged engaged citizenship – in the affairs of the university and in global issues such as poverty, violence, and racism. It worked through the Canadian Federation of Students to

··· STUDENT COMMUNICATORS ···

lobby on national student issues, especially the rising costs of attending university.

Students provided a multitude of strong voices on campus, not always harmoniously perhaps but vigorously. The old "master-disciple" ("master-servant"?) relationships, inherited from centuries of academic life were slowly dissolving. It was not an easy process for all faculty members, but, like the tides, it was hardly resistible.

In 1990, the Faculty of Graduate Studies marked its twenty-fifth anniversary. It was serving nearly 1,400 graduate students, about 600 more than in 1980.[15] There would be nearly 1,800 in 2000. Some eighteen new graduate programmes were developed during the nineties, most within departments, some in interdisciplinary fields. Four reasons largely explain the growth. More students pursued graduate training for its own sake. More employers demanded it. Several departments needed graduate students for teaching and research. And, most gratifying of all, many UVic faculty members were becoming celebrated for their work within and without the university; they were in demand.

The growing numbers of graduate students stabilized the development of the Graduate Students' Society (GSS), which had been formally organized in 1984, though informally its forerunner had been active since the later 1960s.[16] The GSS enriched the graduate student experience at UVic and promoted student interests within the Faculty of Graduate Studies and the university generally. In the late 1990s, its work was greatly enhanced when, through special grants from the government and UVic (and a generous contribution from the Halpern family), a graduate student building was constructed beside the Student Union Building. An attractive building with inviting patios, it quickly became popular for lunches, GSS activities, and late afternoon informal seminars (as some called them).

Much student life, graduate and undergraduate, was simultaneously transformed by the construction of residences. More students were on campus during the evenings and on weekends. Students from the local area also tended to be there longer in the average day. UVic was becoming less of a "drop-in" university. To quote David Clode, who first arrived as a student in 1968 and worked for over thirty years with and for students,[17] UVic, in the sixties was, in the evenings, "like an abandoned aerodrome from one of those 1950s horror films ... and on the weekends the place was just totally deserted."[18] By the 1990s, evening classes were numerous and larger. The athletic facilities were in constant use. Cinecenta, the most consistently interesting movie house in the city, attracted good crowds. The Faculty of Fine Arts presented rich and increasingly professional theatre and music programmes. Visiting speakers, many invited through the Lansdowne programme, and UVic faculty through a new Provost's Lecture Series (established by Vice-President Scully in 1993), gave public talks in the evening.

And, at about nine o'clock, groups started moving from the library to the pub (though a dedicated few might have arrived earlier). The isolation originally associated with being in "the wilds of Gordon Head" was becoming less evident; it was difficult to think UVic was the deserted set of a horror movie.

Students were also becoming more involved in the community, particularly through the burgeoning co-op option, which expanded rapidly in large part because of the work of Graham Branton, the programme's director from 1978 to 1995. By 1990, its seventeen programmes were serving 1,400 students annually; by 1996, when co-op celebrated its twentieth anniversary, it was organizing over 2,000 placements annually. Some co-op students (particularly in law and business) went elsewhere in Canada or to other countries.[19] The largest numbers of co-op students came from the sciences and business, but there were growing numbers from philosophy, history, and the arts, where the connection was perhaps less obvious.

Student life, however, was most affected by what many carried by 2000 – their laptops. Despite initial reservations, faculty usually allowed them to be brought into classrooms – large notebooks, long the badge of studenthood, gradually disappeared. Students accessed vast quantities of information previously difficult to locate on their own and could easily impress by the facts they knew. They could communicate easily (perhaps too easily?) with others; they became part of different online communities, near and far. Sometimes, it is even alleged, one or two students at the back of classrooms used them to play games when lectures palled. They also made plagiarism easier, thereby robbing some students of the supreme accomplishment of their academic careers. Like all the great communication revolutions from the printing press onward, the computing revolution had mixed effects.

....

STUDENT SERVICES

Students are always changing. At any given time, they can be facing one or more major transitions in their lives, many of them invigorating and enjoyable, others rather unpleasant. Growing from adolescence to adulthood, moving away from home, learning how to do laundry (finding a drawer to put it

The students in Fine Arts will search for employment where they can, and here representatives of all the faculty's main programmes perform for any passer-by who might be on the beach. No record was kept as to whether any bookings were achieved.

91

Promoting healthy choices among students.

in?), learning more independently, staying out (and sleeping in) late, assuming responsibilities if one had a family, confronting personal limitations or uncertainties, and, if older, enrolling under pressures to expedite career changes – these are just some of the transitions students typically undergo. When universities are small, they can readily help people navigate some of these transitions. As they expand, size and anonymity limit possibilities – and, indeed, raise questions about how much responsibility an institution should and can shoulder.

Somewhere in the 1970s and 1980s, UVic had ceased to be a village. It had become a sizeable town populated by highly transitory people, with all that means for interpersonal relationships and public wellness. By the 1990s, for example, security – for faculty, staff, and visitors as well as students – had become problematic. In the mid-nineties, UVic undertook a safety audit, gathering views from over 1,500 people on campus. It added brighter lights along its pathways and installed security phones. It hired more security officers and organized security walks for evening students. It sponsored the UVic Safety Troupe to provide humorous but pointed skits in the University Centre, reminding people about the everyday risks around them. There were troubling edges to UVic's comfortable world.

The university significantly expanded the services it offered students, many of them overseen by the Division of Student and Ancillary Services, directed by Jim Griffith and David Clode. Among other services, it offered a highly successful Peer Helping Centre where students assisted fellow students facing writing, drug dependency, alcoholism, and financial problems. It developed welcoming weeks for new students.

UVic Health Services, established in 1969, grew steadily under the leadership of Dr Jack Petersen (he retired in 1999). It too felt greater pressures – or perhaps found itself coping with more acknowledged problems. Partly, though, students had more health issues because they travelled more. Various communicable diseases, notably hepatitis B and HIV, while far from common, were frequent enough that a policy had to be developed in 1996. Changing government treatments for people with emotional problems meant that UVic had to deal with the consequences. More students experienced stress and depression associated with financial as well as personal problems. The end of term, when papers were due, exams were looming, and funds were dwindling, was especially problematic.

One way to improve one's health was through increased physical activity. UVic increased access to recreational athletic facilities, not easy given its expanding physical education programmes and involvement in intercollegiate athletics. The situation improved, however, after 1991 when the university purchased land and buildings owned by St Michaels University School near one of UVic's main gates. UVic converted them largely into a facility for general recreational use and sports clubs, thanks partly to the personal interest and financial contribution of Ian Stewart, the chair of the Board of Governors.

During the 1990s, some students, staff, and faculty became increasingly concerned about daycare. The first campus day-care had been developed in 1969 by volunteers from the three groups and was housed in rooms provided by the university in the military huts. By 1990, the demand had exceeded the supply. The graduating class of that year drew attention to the problem by donating $15,000 for a new daycare building. Other gifts followed. In 1997, many groups and individuals undertook a special campaign to raise $600,000 for a new building. Their success, added to grants from the BC govern-ment, the UVSS, the UVic capital budget, and a generous gift from the Harry Lou-Poy family, made construction possible. The building opened in 2001.

During the 1990s UVic also responded to the spiritual needs and issues of students, faculty, and the community. It provided facilities for more chaplains (by 2000, there were nineteen, more than double the number in 1990).[20] In 1997, UVic adopted a policy that accommodated the special reli-gious beliefs of an increasingly pluralistic student body. The

left | During the 1980s, as pressures on students mounted, the Interfaith Chaplaincy (originally called the Ecumenical Chaplaincy when it was established in 1977) grew steadily under the leadership of (L–R): Rev. Marlowe Anderson (Anglican), Rev. Clare Holmes (United Church), and Father Leo Roberts (Roman Catholic), shown here with student intern pastor Les Skonnord.

right | One change on campus appreciated by all was the development of Finnerty Gardens. Originally located on 1.5 acres inside the Ring Road, it soon expanded, with the help of many volunteers, to a large area across the Ring Road, one that was also more suitable for rhododendrons, the most spectacular of the gardens' species. One of the volunteers was Dr Herman Vaartnou, here shown discussing the rhodos with Friends of Finnerty Gardens, a group that, among other activities, assists in the development of the gardens. Vaartnou developed over fifty new species of rhododendrons, many of which can be found in the gardens.

Interfaith Chapel, constructed in 1986 through donations from alumni and friends of the university, was used more extensively – a quiet place located in a beautiful space beside Finnerty Gardens.

....

THE DEVELOPMENT OF THE CAMPUS

By 2000 UVic was scarcely recognizable from what it had been forty years earlier. The swampy areas had disappeared. Buildings, lawns, athletic fields and gardens had replaced farmers' fields. The skylarks had left, relocating, like many other Victorians, to the available lands of the Saanich Peninsula. A few military huts remained, but they too were a disappearing species, their origins so little comprehended that students would ask: what were they? Why were they the same size? Why the rather drab colours? A few recognized barracks from the old war movies; one wag even suggested that momentarily young "Brits" would pour out the doors, heading for their Spitfires to save London.[21] They never did.

There were more new buildings aside from those constructed for students and daycare. The main new buildings were for the faculties of Human and Social Development, Fine Arts, Visual Arts, Engineering, and Business and Economics. Major renovations were undertaken in the MacLaurin Building, the McPherson Library, and the Cornett Building. Most of the construction conformed generally in style and colours to the existing main buildings; architecturally, UVic buildings possessed a kind of consistency about them – they were on a human scale, did not exceed five stories, and were adorned by shrubs and plants. There were places for art and murals drawn from the holdings of the University of Victoria Art Collections. Totem poles adorned special places. Some even claimed that UVic had become an "outdoor art gallery" – appropriate enough, given the university's responsibility to encourage and preserve artistic expression.

As important as the new buildings were, their impact on faculty and staff, as with the students, was dwarfed by computing. The mainframe continued to evolve, but increasingly powerful desktop computers and local networks were replacing it. Faculty and staff argued vigorously about alternative software packages – with the passion and convictions once reserved for politics and religion. Computer-trained secretaries, usually young, were suddenly central figures in offices – historic hierarchies were disrupted.

Academically, computers made it much easier to accumulate and manipulate data. Faculty members speeded up their work, produced papers more easily, and worked with others, near and far, more conveniently. UVic's expanding engagement with computers, perhaps most dramatically observable in the sciences and engineering, was recognized in 2009, when the

above | Sometimes, with so much construction occurring at UVic, it seemed to go on forever. Finally, though, the causes of the seemingly slow pace were explained.

facing page | Another welcome change was the addition of Mystic Vale. It is a forested ravine featuring Douglas and Grand fir, west coast maple and Arbutus trees. It was added in 1993. Together with nearby Haro woods, it is being preserved in its natural state as much as possible, given its great popularity for walkers and their illegally present dogs.

university successfully competed in the Canada Foundation for Innovation to manage the province's first "super computer." Two hundred times more powerful than the strongest personal computers, it could perform the modeling, simulation, and data analysis needed for the scientific examination of galaxies, high-energy physics, climate modeling, and DNA sequencing.

On another level, increased computing use meant that secretaries and departmental administrators took over many tasks previously performed centrally. Considerable routine work was decentralized; office workloads and responsibilities changed. More reports became necessary. The registration process was revolutionized; long student lineups, the ritualized opening of each term, were much shorter by 2000. Email burst on unsuspecting users, consuming hours but expediting communications among students and colleagues. Computer malfunctioning became the standard reason for tardy papers by delinquent faculty – replacing (as was the case for students) mysterious illnesses and slow snail mail.

Whether computing deepened human relationships is not so obvious. The essential image of the computing age is a person isolated in front of a machine, the location indiscernible, community associations unclear, engagements transitory and probably soon forgotten.

....

THE CHANGING WAYS OF KNOWING

One of the most impressive aspects of UVic in the 1990s was the growth in research activities fostered by a growing support system developed by the associate vice-presidents, John Jackson and Alex McAuley. Professors and students in many different fields explored new and old topics in many new ways. Old networks often became less important, disciplinary boundaries less restrictive. A few of the boundaries even disappeared, most notably the grand old associations housed in the Faculty of Arts and Science, home for the divisions of Humanities, Social Science, and Science.

By the 1990s, whatever intellectual and political ties binding the three divisions together were loosening. New faculties, jostling for influence and relating to arts and science differently, were pressuring for equal status. The essence of the old relationships within Arts and Science (which arguably had been more assumed than defined) was disappearing. Its role at the centre of the university was fading: there were other and compelling ways of knowing. Moreover, all three divisions had their own financial pressures, new interests, faculty relationships, and differing (often competing) ambitions. They separated in 1997 and became faculties, logically enough perhaps, but for many the separation meant the loss of regularized exchanges across faculties, not an insignificant consequence. What the ancient Greeks had called the agora – a business but also a social and political meeting place – was no longer so easily located at UVic.

The flourishing of research at UVic in the 1990s stemmed from several different developments:

- The maturing of faculty members hired earlier.
- The addition of several outstanding researcher/teachers during the 1990s.
- The growth of graduate programmes.
- Expanding growing administrative support for research, particularly through increasing understanding of the operations of the national research funding organizations.
- Flexibility in teaching assignments that allowed for more research time.
- Increased funding from research councils and foundations.

The growth in research can be categorized in three ways: that undertaken by prominent research networks, old and new; that created by new centres; and that conducted by individuals. What follows is a highly selective and limited sampling of the many remarkable research accomplishments at UVic during the 1990s.

One of the most powerful developing networks was concerned with oceans, though that interest soon included the land (particularly the land adjoining the oceans) and climate. The School of Earth and Ocean Sciences (SEOS) was established in 1991. Its first director was Chris Barnes. The school grew rapidly, recruiting "world class people" and drawing out "some of the best people in existing departments."[22] It quickly became known for its path-breaking work in ocean sciences, earth sciences, and climate studies. In 1991, it joined with other universities in exploring the ocean floor along BC's coast undertaken by a remarkable vessel, the *Resolution*, which boasted a derrick some sixty-one metres long!

As the decade passed, UVic scientists, within and without SEOS, made UVic a world centre for ocean studies: for example, Chris Garrett on ocean processes and Verena Tunnicliffe on deepwater life. A selected group of researchers, led by Rosemary Ommer, moved the focus onshore and, in collaboration with researchers in Newfoundland and Labrador, developed a large research programme called Coasts Under Stress. They explored the challenges facing many coastal communities experiencing environmental shifts, declining resources, and global warming.

Another new development was the Centre on Aging. Even though Victoria was a "natural laboratory for the whole country in terms of the social, health, political, and economic issues" confronting seniors, David Hultsch and Lou Costa (also dean of Social Science) in Psychology and Elaine

left | Chris Barnes, a principal leader in the development of ocean research at UVic. Photo credit Diana Nethercott.

right | Verena Tunnicliffe, from the Department of Biology and the School of Earth and Ocean Sciences, holds the Canada Research Chair in Deep Ocean Research. She explores the ecology of unusual deepwater ecosystems off the coast of British Columbia, notably those associated with hydrothermal vents and subsea volcanoes. In the picture above she stands before pictures of some of the equipment she uses in her research and some of the underwater communities she studies.

Gallagher in Nursing worked for a decade before it opened in 1990. Then it faced a serious challenge finding a director,[23] a not uncommon problem with new centres, one that typically requires a determined, sustained, and patient search for a committed, informed, and experienced administrative leader. Ultimately, UVic located Neena Chappell, a Cape Bretoner who had headed a similar centre in Manitoba. She possessed a clear vision of what the centre should be and the proactive perseverance to make it happen. She (and the colleagues and students who became associated with her) mingled a rigorous research agenda with the genuine engagement of local seniors – not always an easy task.

Another key expanding area was Aboriginal studies. The School of Child and Youth Care developed a university degree programme, The Career Ladder Project, with the Meadow Lake Tribal Council in Saskatchewan to improve how Aboriginal children were taught. It subsequently modified the programme to meet the needs, while respecting the local cultures, of BC's Indigenous peoples. The School of Public Administration, supported by the Faculty of Law, developed a programme in Aboriginal governance led initially by Frank Cassidy, a dedicated adult educator. Cassidy devoted many years to its development, working particularly with First Nations in Northern British Columbia – and not a little with colleagues at UVic. In

1997, Taiaiake Alfred, from the Kahnawake Territory of the Mohawk Nation, joined the programme, bringing with him a passionate commitment to increasing Aboriginal control over their lives. The programme attracted significant numbers of Aboriginal – and other – students to its courses and its essential messages.

UVic expanded its First Nations connections in many other ways. The Anthropology Department had long traditions of such involvement and they deepened during the decade. It expanded its work with Indigenous peoples in the Interior and along the coast to document their history, explore their lifestyles, and understand the transitions through which they were going. Christine Welsh, an award-winning Métis documentary filmmaker joined Women's Studies. The Linguistics Department continued to build on its international reputation for preserving Indigenous languages, strongly motivated by the serious decline in numbers of native speakers. Sociology and Social Work examined social issues confronting First Nations people in their home communities and in urban settings. Kathleen Absolon in Social Work, the first tenure-track First Nations person appointed at UVic, organized major conferences for Aboriginal women coping with the problems many of them faced. The Law Faculty explored Aboriginal legal concerns and trained cadres of First Nations students for work associated with treaties, land claims, restorative justice, and differing legal traditions. The Faculty

left | Neena Chappell, the builder of the Centre on Aging at UVic.

centre | Frank Cassidy (second from left) meeting with First Nations leaders from Northern British Columbia.

right | Taiaiake Alfred, the director of the Indigenous Governance Programme.

··· INDIGENOUS OUTDOOR CARVINGS OF UVIC: THE LEGACY ···

of Education developed creative educational practices among Indigenous peoples in both remote and urban places. The History Department added courses and appointments that meant it could more accurately reflect the Aboriginal dimensions of the Canadian and American past. The university opened an Aboriginal Liaison Office, headed by William White, to help Aboriginal students adapt to university.

During the 1980s, UVic had expanded its research and teaching in health studies, particularly in the training of health care professionals. A UVic report in 1991 summarized the approach that had evolved. It emphasized preventative medicine, interdisciplinary perspectives, self-help strategies, and expanded research.[24] The report led to collaboration with UBC and Simon Fraser University in the pursuit of funding for health promotion centres. That collaboration was successful. UVic's centre, through the efforts of Helen Rabinovitch and Marilyn Walker, worked with youth at risk, HIV/

left | William White, Aboriginal Liaison Office, who helped many First Nations students adapt successfully to UVic during the 1990s and the early years of the twenty-first century.

right | When the Sto:lo First Nation in the Fraser Valley invited the History Department in 1997 to bring graduate students into their community to help with some research questions, it seemed unlikely. It seems even more unlikely, a dozen years later, that the programme is still very active and shows no sign of slowing. Operating every second year, it has produced fifty-five field reports, a dozen theses, parts of books, and a special issue of a journal. The Ethnohistory Field School with the Sto:lo Nation remains one of UVic's most enduring partnerships with a First Nation, as this photo from 2007 demonstrates.

AIDS sufferers, sex workers, and the homeless in Victoria, all groups needing better health services.

There were several other important emerging concentrations of research and teaching strengths, such as: the Centre for Studies in Religion and Society, established in 1992 under the leadership of Harold Coward, which provided an academic and increasingly rich perspective on major religious issues; a programme in Contemporary Social and Political Thought, organized in 1991 by professors in Political Science, Sociology, and Philosophy; European Studies, owing much to the work of Amy Verdun in Political Science, became a focus for new ways of thinking about Europe; legal studies, including legal history, women and the law, and law and public policy; the study of multiracial relationships in Vancouver and Victoria by the Institute for Dispute Resolution and Women's Studies; "public history" within the History Department; interdisciplinary programmes in Canadian Arts and Film Studies and in Cultural Resource Management, both in Fine Arts; the study of youth violence in local schools by the School of Child and Youth Care and the Faculty of Education; racism in Canada and the modern world by several researchers/teachers – Yvonne Martin-Newcombe

left | President David Strong signs an agreement with Bishop Remi De Roo for the permanent loan of the Seghers Collection to the University of Victoria Library. It consists of over 4,000 volumes in several languages and covers a rich diversity of topics from the sixteenth to the nineteenth centuries. Charles John Seghers was bishop of Victoria from 1873 to 1886. Harold Coward, the founder of the Centre for Studies in Religion and Society, is standing behind Bishop De Roo and President Strong, 30 March 1995.

right | The Centre for Studies in Religion and Society World Partnership Walk, 2007.

(Education), Rennie Warburton (Sociology), and Phyllis Senese (History). The list could be longer …

At the same time, many older research concentrations continued to thrive. UVic's involvement with TRIUMF expanded considerably when the Meson Facility on the UBC campus received a $700 million upgrade so it could produce kaons (subatomic particles) on a mass scale, thereby enabling UVic scientists to continue the work for which they had become well-known.

Finally, often very quietly, numerous individuals made remarkable research contributions. A few examples – from very many that could be selected – suggests the strength and range of this kind of enquiry:

- Michael Best (English) developed a software package for innovative teaching and research about Shakespeare, his plays, his life, and his times.
- David Lai (Geography) received the Order of Canada for his work on and with the Chinese community in Victoria and British Columbia.

left | Tri-University Meson Facility (TRIUMF).

right | David Lai, whose work with Chinese-Canadians since the 1960s achieved national and international recognition and contributed greatly to our understanding of the Chinese experience in Victoria.

left | John Oleson, whose work in historical archaeology has been widely recognized internationally and has inspired many students since the 1970s.

right | Nancy Turner, an ethnobotanist in Environmental Studies, one of UVic's most honoured teachers and researchers. Among the many recognitions she has received: she is a member of the Order of British Columbia, the Order of Canada, and the Royal Society of Canada. Here she is teaching a class about First Nations culture and local indigenous plants.

- John Oleson (Classics) gained an international reputation for his work on ancient technology, particularly ships, harbours, and water-supply systems at the site of Humayma, ancient Hawara, a small caravan stop in Jordan's southern desert.
- Angus McLaren (History) somehow managed to make the histories of sex and murder interesting.
- Steve Lonergan (Geography) gained international recognition for his work on the environment and security.
- Frances Ricks (Child and Youth Care) explored issues associated with equity and ethics, much of it "on the ground" in Aboriginal villages, the Victoria area, and on the UVic campus.
- John Tucker (English) in collaboration with W.D. Valgardson (Writing) made UVic a centre for spreading the knowledge about Iceland through lectures, film festivals, art exhibitions, musical performances, and symposia on Icelandic topics sponsored by the Beck Trust.

- Jack Littlepage (Biology), working with the Canadian International Development Agency, helped reformulate the Brazilian fishing industry to help fishing communities become more prosperous.
- Jan Zwicky (Philosophy), a highly respected teacher of philosophy and an accomplished musician, won a Governor-General's award for her poetry.
- Nancy Turner (Environmental Studies), one of the world's foremost ethnobotanists, became a celebrated and much-appreciated researcher into native plants, and her collaboration with First Nations people became a model for others to follow. She received many awards for her work and for the spirit that motivated it, including several awards from her professional colleagues, the Order of British Columbia, and, ultimately, the Order of Canada.
- Cecilia Benoit (Sociology) gained national prominence through her work on women's health and the environment.
- Stephen Scobie (English), a poet, is also an expert on Scottish writers and Bob Dylan.
- Colin Bennett (Political Science) became widely known for his expertise in privacy legislation.
- Martin Collis (Physical Education) is a very popular expert and speaker on workplace wellness, mingling humour and music with strong messages on lifestyle and stress management.

In fine arts, "research" often takes different forms and is represented usually in performance and community activities. Under the leadership of the dean of Fine Arts, Anthony Welch, the faculty enjoyed remarkable success. Each of its schools – Visual Arts, Theatre, Music, Writing, and History in Art – flourished; each possessed faculty members with international accomplishments and excellent reputations as teachers. The UVic symphony and choir prospered under the leadership of János Sándor. The Chamber Singers entertained in nearby venues and in other countries. New and prominent faces were added to the faculty, including Mavor Moore, appointed jointly with the Faculty of Humanities, who brought some fifty years of experience at the heart of Canada's cultural industries; Alexandra Browning-Moore,

Martin Collis

Stephen Scobie

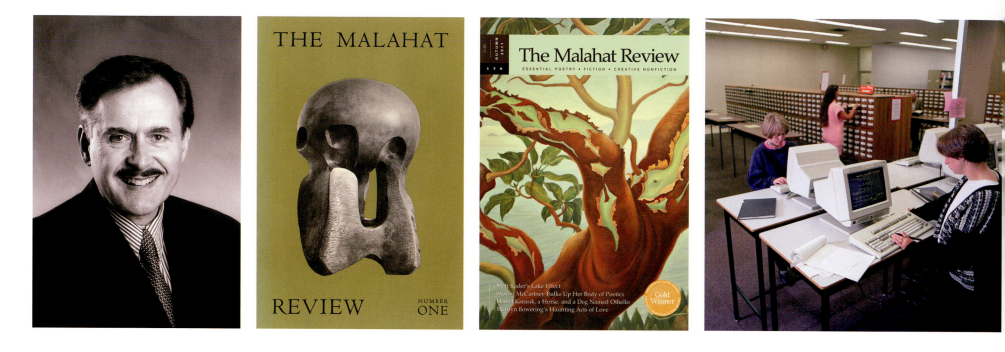

left | Anthony Welch, dean of Fine Arts, 1985–98.

centre | Ever since it began in 1967, *The Malahat Review* (the covers of its first and latest issues are pictured here) has made a major contribution to literary studies in British Columbia and Canada.

right | The McPherson Library in 1991.

a soprano with a very distinguished singing career in both the United Kingdom and Canada; and the Lafayette String Quartet, four celebrated musicians who continued their concert programmes while instructing students in the violin, cello, and viola. Lorna Crozier, one of Canada's finest poets, joined the Department of Writing in 1991.

As research flourished at UVic in the 1990s, the library became an even more important resource. Under the leadership of the university librarian, Marnie Swanson, appointed in 1988, it was transformed. UVic had always supported the library comparatively well, and its first librarian, Dean Halliwell, had overseen the development of a strong collection for a university of UVic's size. By the late 1980s, though, the library, which used its own systems, was struggling to adapt to the technological changes then transforming libraries. It had to be reorganized to meet current needs and to move swiftly into new forms of automation. Those were the challenges that Swanson, her colleagues, and a very active advisory committee undertook during the 1990s. It was hard work.

If the central mission of a university can be reduced to an unshakable respect for knowledge and cultural understandings and the passionate pursuit of them, then UVic was reaching new levels as the nineties ended. It had become an important Canadian and international centre for research in many different forms, a place of some considerable, if not yet widely recognized, significance.

....

THE CHANGING FACULTY AND STAFF EXPERIENCES

UVic faculty changed remarkably during the 1990s. Almost 300 faculty members were hired, mostly to replace retiring professors. It is a mark of the effectiveness of appointment procedures developed over the preceding decade that this expansion created few tensions; in the past, at UVic and elsewhere, such rapid growth had frequently caused turmoil.

That did not mean there were not tensions. Many of them came from how faculty members – whether old or new – related to each other. They involved practices and attitudes, conscious and unconscious, associated with issues related to gender, race, and disabilities. In part, the issues emerged because of concerns of people on campus; in part, they developed because the federal government in the late 1980s adopted the Federal Contractors Program, which sought to ensure better and more equal opportunity for four groups – women, Native peoples, persons with disabilities, and visible minorities – employed through federal funding. UVic could not be exempt.

The discussions soon focused on gender equality. In the spring of 1990, when the percentage of permanent female faculty members was below 20 per cent, the Board of Governors adopted an equity policy. It adopted a moderate form of affirmative action, directed particularly at departments where one could reasonably expect more women to be employed. It did not require quotas but asked units on campus to develop effective plans appropriate to their disciplines or areas of work, to assure women applicants for positions that they would be welcomed and treated fairly.

This request triggered intense debates in some departments and units; for some at UVic, it seemed like a form of discrimination. It engendered discussions over how faculty search committees should welcome female applicants, take into account different career paths, and assess feminist forms of scholarship. It stimulated discussions on gender relations generally on campus, including considerations of many aspects of life in departments and administrative units – a complex and often uncomfortable process.

The most prominent gender issue commenced in 1992 when the Department of Political Science created a committee called the Committee to Make the Department More Supportive of Women (informally, the Chilly Climate Committee). Chaired by a new faculty member, Somer Brodribb, its name defined its mandate. Her report, prepared with the help of five female graduate students, was tabled in March 1993. It harshly criticized the situation in the department for female students and faculty and for feminist enquiry. It alleged that some (unidentified) males in the department were guilty of various kinds of harassment. Deeply aggrieved by those charges, the men in the department responded angrily. Subsequent meetings demonstrated that discussion and conciliation were impossible. Whatever the climate before, it had certainly become "chillier." It was also immediately a national issue: political science departments at other universities (UBC, Manitoba, and Western Ontario) were undertaking similar projects. The Canadian Association of University Teachers become involved in encouraging better gender relations within Canadian universities. What happened at UVic had an immediate impact elsewhere.

The dispute festered for a year, impeding the work of the department and dividing the university, not just the department. In late 1993, the university developed a harassment policy, including procedures to implement it.[25] The intent was to respond to some of the issues evident in the Political Science dispute and, as the board requested, "ensure that the university provide a safe and supportive environment for women."[26] The administration also appointed an advisor to the president on equity and officials to deal with harassment issues – Norma Mickelson (1986–91), Sheila Devine and Barbara Whittington (1991–96), Linda Sproule-Jones (1996–2008), Susan Shaw (1994–2003), and Cindy Player (2004–present).

As for the Political Science issue, the president in late 1993 established a committee, consisting of Beth Bilson from the University of Saskatchewan (and the provincial Labour Relations Board) and Thomas R. Berger from the BC Supreme Court, to investigate. Their 1994 report challenged both sides in the dispute, questioning some of the methodology of the Brodribb report, and criticizing how male members of the department had responded to it. It recommended appointing a female chair, appealed for the more careful use of language when discussing such issues, advocated carrying forward systematically the work that the Brodribb committee had begun, and suggested modifications of the UVic tenure document's ethical conduct section.

The university administration accepted the report, though some (on the two main sides in the Political Science Department) questioned it seriously. Tensions did subside in the department somewhat but did not disappear; they would be felt for years. Court cases did not proceed. Brodribb and another female instructor, Kathy Teghtsoonian, transferred to other departments. The graduate students involved moved on. Other women faculty members were added to the department. In 1996, James Tully from McGill University, one of Canada's most distinguished academics, arrived as the department's new chair. He had an international reputation in political theory but also extensive expertise in feminist and minority issues, valuable assets under the circumstances.

In total, the experience left deep scars on all of those directly involved, shaping careers and undermining reputations. It demonstrated the seriousness and complexity of such issues and arguably showed the risks of self-analysis (as opposed to external assessments). It nevertheless contributed to serious efforts to establish procedures that would help deal with such issues. It meant (perhaps above all) that gender concerns would be a part of life at UVic indefinitely. Open, mutually respectful workplaces cannot be created by fiat or even through administrative vigilance, though they can help. Ultimately it is a matter for individual responsibility within supportive communities – a responsibility no one can (or should seek to) avoid.

During the 1990s, UVic also began to appraise more carefully the services it provided people with disabilities. It held symposia exploring the challenges confronting them. It held highly publicized days when administrators, teachers, staff, and students travelled around the campus in wheelchairs or with eyes covered to better realize the challenges involved.

left | Vice-President Sam Scully sees first-hand how the university can improve the ways in which it accommodates people in wheelchairs.

right | Some of the people who helped make UVic function smoothly – the Facilities Management team, undated.

With government assistance, UVic renovated older buildings to improve wheelchair access and ensured that its new buildings served people with disabilities more effectively. In 1995, it opened a Resource Centre for Students with a Disability, so as to help with essay preparation, Braille translations, classroom participation, and fairer examination process.

These efforts demonstrated once again that operating a university was becoming more complicated. So too did relations with non-faculty staff members. Most of the staff at UVic had been organized into two CUPE locals in the mid-1960s. Between that time and the 1990s, negotiations were generally amicable, issues were settled without strikes or even acrimonious debate. During the 1990s, tensions began to grow, partly because people long involved in the negotiations had retired, partly because of the emergence of pay equity as a difficult issue, and partly because UVic was an increasingly complex organization. During the 1990s, the unions and the university undertook the lengthy and complex process of developing a system to ensure "equal pay for equal work." It was a challenging task.

The decade also saw the organization of a Professional Employees Association and the union for teaching assistants (CUPE 4163). They were formed because of the impact of funding cuts in the preceding years and the increasing complexity of their relationships with the steadily growing UVic. By 1997, informal ways of dealing with such issues were no longer satisfactory.

....

RELATIONS WITH COMMUNITIES

In its first decade or so, when UVic was more like a village and the ideal of the Liberal Arts largely dominated, it was customary to think that "town" and "gown" were essentially separate – customary but probably never really true: public universities can never be significantly aloof from the communities in which they exist. By the 1990s, UVic itself was more like a town with greater segmentation and a much larger and transient population. The informal bonds that had once been strong within the college were dissipating.

The connections with nearby communities, however, multiplied and deepened. The most obvious and vital connections, of course, were through students, about 40 per cent of whom came from nearby communities. The students were increasingly diverse in objectives and backgrounds, therefore expanding UVic's local connections. The development of the professional schools, for example, brought people on campus with immediate, specific career goals and with different life experiences. The difference was noticeable in nearly all classrooms.

··· BUILDINGS, 1990–2000: THE LEGACY ···

The growing community demand led UVic to expand its evening, spring, and summer offerings. The UVic presence in the community – and its impact on it – was no longer compacted into two thirteen-week semesters, the traditional Canadian academic year. The campus was seldom quiet. Its constant bustle spilled over into the nearby communities, a source for much economic activity.

The university contributed in other ways. Research activities significantly affected how UVic related to nearby local communities. Some of it, for example, possessed economic possibilities. In 1991, UVic established a stand-alone entity, the Victoria Innovation and Development Corporation (IDC). Its purposes were to assist UVic research and to help university research-ers develop enterprises, not only in the sciences, computing, and business, where such entrepreneurship might be readily facilitated, but also in the arts, linguistics, law, writing, and social sciences as well. According to David Strong, it was a way in which the university could make "more of its discov-eries, new knowledge, and special expertise available to the public."[27] During its first five years, IDC (largely with funds raised off campus) helped create "eight spin-off companies, invested in almost twenty projects and twenty-four patents, fielded more than 200 inquiries from students, faculty and staff, and directly benefited graduate and post-doctoral students by provid-ing research grants to UVic professors."[28] The impact on the local economy was significant and it was growing.

Other research by students and teachers focused on the Greater Victoria region in more traditional ways. It explored such topics as the needs of seniors, environmental issues, poverty, homelessness, economic trends, the immigrant experience, and local food production. Researchers (especially students) explored issues around transportation, housing, waste manage-ment, pollution, and energy production. These interests directly affected UVic by reinforcing concerns already evident on campus. The result was that, during the 1990s, UVic embarked on a series of changes improving recycling practices, providing bicycle racks, facilitating greater bus use, and encouraging car pools.

UVic people during the 1990s were engaged in many aspects of the public life and the community debates of the region. Martin Segger, from the Maltwood Gallery, a man who played many roles at UVic, was an unofficial ambassador with significant contacts throughout the city (and beyond) in the heritage and cultural communities. Neil Swainson (Oak Bay councilor), Martin Segger (Victoria alderman, then council member), and David Turner (mayor of Victoria) were involved in politics, as was Andrew Petter, a member of the Legislature and attorney-general. Several UVic faculty members were prominent media commentators, including Ron Cheffins (Law), Norman Ruff (Political Science), and Michael Prince (Human and

Social Development). The professional faculties – Law, Business, Education, and Engineering, in particular – had multi-faceted, important and continuous relationships with communities. The Division of Continuing Studies specifically developed programmes to meet the needs of various community groups. Students from many departments, through co-op terms and programme placements became common in the community. Many students volunteered their time, a generous exercise in public responsibility. In 1996, UVic started "Blue and Gold Awards" honouring outstanding contributions by students to the university and the community: activities such as volunteering at the Cancer Society, hospitals, recreation centres, United Way, and relief fundraising. Campus radio, though targeting its programmes to specific audiences, was a voice for alternative ways to understand and to criticize, but also to enjoy, the contemporary world.

All of these developments meant that more funds were always needed – to provide financial support for students, special projects, university infrastructure, research development, exchange agreements, additions to the library. The list seemed to grow with each passing month. One way to find support for them was to expand the UVic Foundation. The foundation had been established in 1954 and it had grown steadily, but not at the rate of some other Canadian university foundations.

In 1992, UVic launched a national campaign (The UVic Challenge), chaired by Donna Thomas from Victoria's investment community, to encourage support for the foundation. The campaign initially featured the Centre for Global Studies and Centre for Innovative Teaching to demonstrate some of the university's new directions. Its initial slogan was, "Big enough to be legitimate and small enough to be effective and responsive." It initially hoped to find funds for new student residences, library additions, new equipment, and an expanded endowment. As the issue of student indebtedness became more pressing, it emphasized the need for enriched bursary and scholarship programmes. The campaign reached out to UVic graduates in communities across Canada. By 1996, it had raised some $25 million for the foundation and had sparked considerable support within the local community.

For many years, a rather eccentric chemist named Dr Zonk entertained young people and their parents as well as students and colleagues at UVic at open houses and many other occasions. Except for garish green hair, doubtless the result of an experiment gone wrong, he bore a striking resemblance to Reg Mitchell, one of the Chemistry Department's very active researchers. Mitchell devoted many hours to popularizing science in Victoria and on Vancouver Island – at science fairs and on a local radio station. He also was deeply committed to the pursuit of academic excellence in the university and for more than two decades served on the Senate in many roles.

The closing ceremonies at the 1994 Commonwealth Games.
Victoria Times Colonist. Photographer John McKay.

Sympathetic community interest was also sparked by the activities of the Speakers' Bureau. The bureau, which had been started in 1980, by 1996 was arranging over 300 talks each term, involving some 120 speakers from UVic, offering talks on over 300 topics. They were speaking to an estimated 10,000 people each year, largely in the Greater Victoria area.[29] They much enlarged UVic's reputation in the community.

The most dramatic connection with the community during the 1990s was the holding of the 1994 Commonwealth Games. Its permanent impact on the university community was the construction of five townhouse complexes, originally to house the athletes, but afterwards to become student housing; the addition of new track facilities; the development of an all-weather field; and the covering of the field hockey pitch with artificial turf. Even more, the games gave the university and the city greatly increased confidence in their capacity to undertake major projects.

One university professor who left the city as the games were ending, watched the conclusion of the marathon live in his hotel room television set in Glasgow, a striking example of how widely UVic was being promoted during the 1990s. Amid challenges and complexities, the university had moved well beyond Gordon Head.

··· ATHLETICS ···

CHANGING CONTOURS, 2000–2013

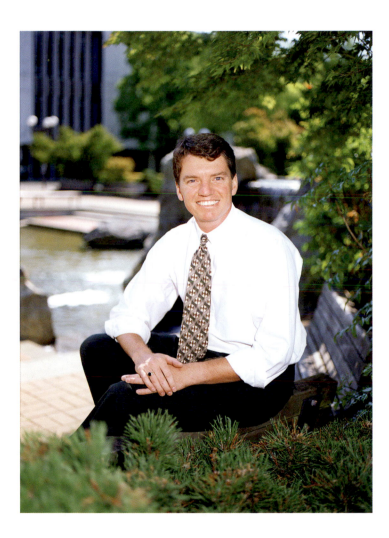

above | David H. Turpin, president, 2000–
Photo: Vince Klassen/*UVic Torch Alumni Magazine*

facing page | Aerial view, 2003.

It was, of course, an honour to have been asked to consider the presidency of another university. But as David Turpin sat in his Queen's University office – and even though he had grown up on Vancouver Island – he, like others in the Canadian university world, had only a general impression of Canada's farthest west university. He probed, therefore, into the data comparing UVic with other Canadian universities on such aspects as research profiles, quality of students, and faculty awards. He was impressed by what he saw and asked, "Why wouldn't I be interested? It was a place that really had the chance to ascend."[1] The previous twenty-five years had witnessed the extensive development of the Gordon Head campus – the maturing of two, arguably three, generations of academics, their accomplishments evident in public records of achievement.

As Turpin investigated further, he sensed a great opportunity. Many of the people he met during the search process expressed uncertainties about the underlying purposes of UVic. What kind of university should it try to be? How should it be different? Such questions suggested openness as to what the future could be, always an exciting prospect for an administrator. Attractive, too, was an ambition that was frequently stated: that UVic should be a university to which people came thoughtfully and with enthusiasm – what is sometimes called a "destination university."

In a sense, his years at Queen's had prepared him for that kind of approach. Queen's had developed where the University of Toronto and McGill were very prominent and, in the case of Toronto, significantly larger. Nevertheless, by insisting on strong teaching, growing strategically, and focusing on some special areas of strength (for example, the public service and the sciences), Queen's had more than held its own. It had become, in fact, a "destination university." For many in Western Canada, for example, from Winnipeg to Victoria and many points in between, the allure of Queen's had been strong, attracting generations of young students to Kingston. It was a university far bigger than purely local support could have made possible. Its branches had spread far beyond its roots.

Expanding UVic's "destination" dimension, therefore, became a priority for the years after 2000. The university increased its student recruitment efforts outside Victoria, particularly in Canada from Quebec westward. As a result, the numbers of non-British Columbia students grew steadily. More students came from the United States, Asia, and Europe, meaning that the students at UVic could learn more about other parts of the world at a time in their lives when such knowledge could be most valuable. By 2012 the campus had developed a distinctively international tone, reflected in different styles of clothes, the issues that emerged, and the languages that could be heard in the student cafeterias.

In 2001, UVic committed to building sufficient residence space over the next three years to accommodate all first year students, a rather ambitious promise since it would mean providing some 600 more residence bedrooms at a cost of over $23 million.[2] Doing so, though, meant that students (and their families) would know that they were coming to a safe and welcoming environment, not unimportant for teenagers living away from home for the first time.

UVic also began to organize more systematically its face to the world. It funnelled all the campus websites and public announcements into a consistent "brand," a kind of uniformity not particularly welcomed by faculty members and units treasuring their individuality. The "branding," however, did provide a single strong set of messages for students carefully comparing universities. It also helped emphasize UVic's growing research accomplishments, continuing commitment to strong teaching, concerns about sustaining collegial relationships on campus, and commitment to preserving pleasant natural surroundings – arguably the most impressive of its positive attributes. The strategy worked. By 2010, UVic had the highest percentage of out-of-province students of any Canadian university west of McGill.

The emphasis on students inevitably buttressed the drive to think about teaching more systematically, a particular concern of the vice-president academic, Jamie Cassels. The Learning and Teaching Centre (LTC) became an increasingly important part of UVic. It emphasized (even more than in the past) one-on-one consultations with faculty members, curriculum design, teaching technologies, speaking skills, and lesson planning. It encouraged international approaches, better evaluation techniques, and improved large

left | Jamie Cassels, vice-president academic and provost, 2001–10, who played a leading role in guiding the significant expansion during the decade. Under his leadership, UVic increased enrolments, especially at the graduate level, as well as student financial assistance.

centre | Ron Lou-Poy, chancellor, 2003–08

right | Murray Farmer, chancellor, 2009–

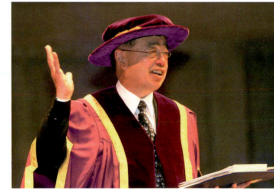

class instruction. It provided special innovation grants for UVic teachers. It stressed the importance of good teaching to recently hired faculty
during their orientation process. It increased its help to graduate students. It
encouraged faculties to develop teaching awards and by 2011 all had done so.
It created a special committee, chaired by Ed Ishiguro, the inaugural master
teacher at the centre, to enhance first-year learning, particularly in large
classes. The LTC became increasingly proactive.

The work of the LTC changed somewhat after Teresa Dawson became director in 2006. It paid more attention to how students learn – the other side
of the education equation. It encouraged faculty members to extend to them
the pleasures of research, to let them benefit by doing more research for and
by themselves. It expanded its helping services, notably in its Writing Centre
and its Mathematics and Statistics Assistance Centre, which became open
to students whether they were struggling to pass or "aiming for an A+."[3] It
worked closely with departments and faculties with curriculum design to
make programmes as integrated and interesting as possible.

At the end of the day, though, while support and policies from the central
administration and the work of the LTC are important, it is up to individual
professors and departments to enhance high teaching standards at UVic.
Only they can really ensure that students are well taught by the best that
UVic can provide. It is not an aspect of the university that can be taken for
granted; it should never be on a back burner.

left | Ed Ishiguro (Biochemistry and Microbiology), a researcher
into problems of resistance to penicillin, and a highly respected
teacher who is the first master teacher in the Learning and Teaching
Centre.

centre | Hamar Foster from the Faculty of Law engaging his
students, the ultimate goal of good teaching.

right | After her term as vice-president academic ended in
2001, Penelope Codding returned to the Chemistry Department
to resume full-time teaching. Though she taught many senior
students, she devoted much of her time to working with others in
revising and revamping the department's introductory courses.
The aim was to communicate the important contributions of
chemistry to the students' lives and to demonstrate how chemists
think and learn, specifically at a molecular level, with models, and
experientially. The courses focused on major themes, such as
"modern materials" and environmental chemistry. They featured
live demonstrations, online weekly quizzes, the use of clickers
to encourage active learning, and animated problem solving. In
the process, she became a role model, and not just for her junior
colleagues and not just in Chemistry.

··· STUDENTS AND THEIR DEPARTMENTS: THE EXAMPLE OF HISTORY ···

The Association of Universities and Colleges of Canada has recently taken up the cause of better teaching. In fact, it has called for the transformation of undergraduate education,[4] echoing Pierre Zundel and Patrick Deane in *University Affairs*: "What is required is a radical re-conceptualizing of the teaching and learning process, where the goal becomes 'helping students learn' rather than 'teaching.' We need to lift ourselves above the instructor-instructed dialectic, and above that equally factitious binary of teaching and research."[5] UVic should particularly be a place where the message is taken to heart; to some extent, at least, it can say it already has.

....

STUDENT ISSUES, STUDENT LIFE

If the nineties saw serious financial issues for students, the first decade of the twenty-first century was worse. In 2002, the provincial government brought the six-year tuition freeze to an end. At UVic, the Board of Governors decided in its budget framework to increase tuition by 30 per cent (or $600 per year for undergraduates and $826 for graduate students). The Board also proposed increasing financial aid and work-study programmes as a way to help students with financial problems. The student leadership nevertheless vigorously opposed the increase, arguing that it was wrong for students to have to begin their working careers with heavy debt loads. By the end of the decade, significant numbers of students were accumulating debts of over $25,000, not a trivial amount. The financial struggles also meant for students more part-time jobs and less ability to give their studies the attention they deserved.

The meeting of the Board to consider the budget framework was on 25 March 2002. It was a chaotic affair. Someone pulled the fire alarm. Sirens and bullhorns interrupted discussions. The Board adjourned to the nearby Business and Economics Building, where they eventually passed it. UVic then began working out how it would be implemented, including finding more funds for bursaries.[6] The issue, however, was not ended and remains a major challenge confronting UVic students, UVic, and Canada itself.

In the years following 2004, an increase in provincial funding for post-secondary institutions significantly increased capacity. This helped address another common problem. The minimum entry grade had soared to over 80 per cent largely because a higher percentage of young people in BC were going to universities. While this trend made it somewhat more likely that only very capable students entered university, it was not a satisfactory cut-off point. University success has never been entirely predictable from high school results. Some students who excel in high school do not prosper in the highly self-reliant environments of universities. Others, with uneven patterns in their high school grades (meaning a lower over-all average) can

121

··· ATHLETICS ···

blossom at university. With an 80 per cent admission standard, they did not have that chance. Students might have low grades in some key grades in high school, such as mathematics and literature, but higher grades in other fields that could be vigorously pursued at university. The disappointments for those not accepted could run deep, especially if they lived close to UVic and particularly wanted to attend it.

Despite such issues, much of student life remained unchanged. Students were as active as they had always been at UVic. The Ian Stewart Complex, the centre for most recreational activities, welcomed a half million users annually, mostly students. They took instructional classes in several sports and enjoyed intramural programmes, outdoor recreation, and racquet sports. They used the field house, dance studio, ice rink, and outdoor pool – as well as the 18,200 square foot fitness and weight centre.

For the exceptional athlete, UVic continued as one of Canada's foremost participants in intercollegiate athletics. By 2011, it had won sixty-eight Canadian university national championships in twelve different sports. It was fourth on the list of all-time winners of national championships among Canadian universities. Nearly 160 Vikes athletes (past and current) from many different sports had competed for Canada at the Olympics; sixty-five of them had brought home medals.

Much student life revolved around the Student Union Building. In addition to its theatre, eating places, and pub, it had several offices and shops devoted to student needs. Stands selling crafts from Canada and southern countries lined the hallways. There were usually information desks on all kinds of student, university, and community events. Music flowed out from the pub (some thought rather loudly) and, on special days, live bands took over temporary stages. Across the road, one of Canada's more successful university bookstores thrived.

While the pleasurable side of student life, as at all times, is obvious, it is also clear that pressures are invariably increasing. Alicia Ulysses, for many years a sessional instructor in the Department of Hispanic and Italian Studies and a close observer of the students she teaches, believes

students today face far more challenges than in previous generations. Once in university, they are expected to have diverse knowledge of technological tools. The competition for post-graduate and professional school entry is fiercer than ever with the realization that a bachelor's is no longer sufficient to obtain a well-paid full-time job. University graduates are expected to have academic knowledge, job and volunteer experience as well as a high level of worldliness and understanding of other cultures and peoples. I feel that university students today work harder than ever.[7]

··· SOME OF THE ARTS AT UVIC ···

The expansion of graduate studies, under the leadership of Dean Aaron Devor and Jamie Cassels, was steady and significant. Graduate students have played vital roles in the development of UVic's research capacity, and not just in the sciences where that connection was long ago recognized. New research methodologies, the policies of funding agencies that encourage the involvement of students in the projects they fund, and the vast quantities of data that are readily available have created endless possibilities for research – and for students to develop new ways of thinking about it. Those circumstances, plus the need for graduate degrees in many professions, explain largely why UVic's graduate programme has developed so quickly.

Between 2000 and 2011, the number of graduate students in the university rose from 1,779 to nearly 2,700. The most substantial increases were in the Faculties of Science and Human and Social Development. Each year, three to six new programmes were added in that time frame. Spread out across the campus, they were and are responses to intellectual pressures from within the university and external demands for expertise. Twelve of the new degrees were at the PhD level, attesting to the deepening of research capacity in the university. Another sixteen were in the process of being considered at the end of 2011.[8]

Computers continued their relentless invasion of the student world. Social media flourished. In the restaurants, students communicated as much through texting messages as by talking to the people sitting beside them. It was an important part of campus life, and particularly obvious in the William C. Mearns Centre for Learning, a substantial addition to the McPherson Library. It was funded by the Mearns family and named for William Mearns, an important figure in UVic's creation. Its impact on students was dramatic.

The Mearns Centre included a "learning commons" and enhanced spaces for archives, video collections, and computing rooms. It glistened behind glass walls, provided computing services that opened up research possibilities that trivialized what had been readily available just a few years earlier, even in much larger institutions. There was space for student assistance in math, sciences, and writing and rooms for collaborative study. Scattered throughout were quiet areas, places for (mostly) muted conversations, and stacks for some two million volumes. It also included a coffee shop, the Bibliocafé, added to enliven the campus atmosphere. It worked; the lineup for designer coffees would never seem to be short. Even the rules changed – students could bring their coffees into the reading rooms – librarians of another age would be scandalized. Nowhere else symbolized more the mingling of traditional and new ways of learning – or more readily demonstrated the excitement it can generate. The building's success is a tribute to the

vision of the Mearns family, Marnie Swanson (the chief librarian), the rest of the library staff, and the university committees responsible for it.

The face of the UVic student body continued to change significantly. After 2000, efforts to welcome students from other lands – and to assist them if assistance was needed – were substantially increased, a particular priority for David Turpin. By 2011, there were more than 1,500 non-Canadian students registered at UVic. More people of colour were evident, as were people from different cultural backgrounds in Asia, Latin America, Africa, and the Middle East. These changes can be seen within the context of UVic's desire to welcome and appropriately assist what were called in the early 2000s "non-traditional" students – defined as "single parents, people with disabilities, gays and lesbians and transgendered persons, mature students, Aboriginals, international and part-time students."[9] UVic is not perfect in how it treats the "non-traditional," but its efforts to be inclusive – to make the student body more reflective of local diversity and international differences – are ongoing and commendable.

left | William C. Mearns (Victoria College 1926–27, UVic Board of Governors 1963–69), whose vision and action was instrumental in the acquisition of the land parcels that now comprise the Gordon Head campus. Photo, courtesy of Craig Mearns

right | Marnie Swanson, university librarian, 1988–2011.

As in the previous decade, UVic between 2000 and 2011 saw remarkable faculty renewal. Some 400 new faculty members were hired, pushing the total to over 800, despite the fact that moving to UVic can be challenging. Victoria is an expensive place in which to live and to begin a career, especially if one carries debts from graduate school or is starting a family. UVic cannot always match the salaries of other universities and to some extent relies on the institutional culture of the university, its vibrant research activities, pleasant students, the attractions of Victoria, and natural beauty to compensate somewhat.[10] It works to some extent: less than 1 per cent of those appointed after 2000 had moved on by 2011.[11]

UVic has made progress in becoming a more equitable place in which to work. A review by the representatives from the federal department of Human Resources and Skills Development Canada in 2003 noted that more women, Aboriginal people, persons with disabilities, and visible minorities had been appointed, and the record has improved as the years have gone by.

Relations between the university and its faculty members have also been cordial and constructive. In 2000, the administration and the Faculty Association concluded a framework agreement governing terms of employment for both faculty members and librarians. In its nearly 200 pages were large portions of the old tenure document, that hardy veteran of continuous updating and campus politics since the 1960s. It addressed such practices as appointment, reappointment, promotion, and tenure procedures, equal opportunity policies, salary, study and parental leave procedures, and financial exigency clauses. Its negotiation was a monumental task, its conclusion a tribute to its chief negotiators, Rodney Symington for the Faculty Association and Lyman Robinson for UVic, and to then vice-president academic Penelope Codding, and Faculty Association president Bill Pfaffenberger.

By 2010, there were over 5,000 employees at UVic, making it the third largest employer in the Capital Regional District. The non-faculty employees were organized into several groups: a union of "inside" workers in offices, technical services and child care (CUPE 951); a union for people who worked on buildings and grounds, food and housing services, athletics and recreation and security (CUPE 917); a union for people who do not hold regular faculty positions but are involved in teaching, such as teaching assistants, lab assistants, language instructors, and sessional instructors (CUPE 4163); and an association for administrative and academic employees (Professional Employees Association).

There has been only one very brief strike in UVic's history, and most negotiations have been settled with little rancour, but the increasing complexity

··· SOME UVIC EMPLOYEES ···

of the university, wage limitations imposed by the government, and the increasing professionalization of the UVic management structure have created some strains that persist. Easy communications seemed more difficult to sustain. In some areas, pay equity was a difficult issue to resolve. The budgetary pressures and government regulations meant limited funds were available for increases in salary and other benefits. Much depended upon the government views of unions since it ultimately approved all settlements. Issues of accommodation became less easily resolved. Pressures on pension funding became worrisome. As people long involved with the unions retired or were replaced – on both sides – the personal relationships were not as close as they had been, and negotiations became more difficult. The underlying issues were the growth of the university in size, and the development of more managerial systems, what the unions and others referred to as the corporatization of the university world, including UVic.[12]

The unions became increasingly involved in building relationships among themselves but also in developing connections with the greater UVic community and with the broader community. They and their members pressed to be recognized as part of the face of UVic, honoured for the contributions they make to the educational programme; the smooth operation of cafeterias, residences, and classrooms; the maintenance of grounds; the functioning of the libraries; and the provision of security. One of the most important examples raised was the role played by secretaries in the operation of departments: Central to any department's effectiveness, they are the "common departmental face" for students. They set the tone for offices all across the campus.

The university provided a range of services for its employees aimed at improving wellness (including the encouragement of exercise), and at providing counseling to help deal with problems that occur: the sometimes hectic pace of change, workplace stress, and conflict resolution. It has introduced the President's Distinguished Services Awards and "Above and Beyond" awards to recognize exceptional contributions. It has encouraged faculties to develop similar awards to recognize exceptional service. Such recognition is important: universities function as well as the communities within them collaborate with each other; they depend on the work done by all of those communities, including those in the workplaces that make good teaching and research possible.

....

RESHAPING THE CAMPUS

As in the 1990s, the UVic campus changed significantly. Several new buildings were constructed. One of them was for the Division of Continuing

The Peter B. Gustavson School of Business has developed a strong reputation as an innovative place to study business, a place that has earned international recognition for its work on entrepreneurship, one that reaches out to the local community in many ways, and that, at the same time, brings a very strong international flavour to the work that it does. Its work has drawn the attention of several people in the region, including two major benefactors, Peter B. Gustavson, after whom the school is named, and Sardul S. Gill, after whom the graduate school of business is named.

Studies, which had grown remarkably in size and stature. By the start of the millennium, it was annually serving some 15,000 people. It had gained an impressive reputation and was garnering many awards from the Canadian Association for University Continuing Education. Its success meant that the university, through the leadership of the dean of Continuing Studies, Wes Koczka, was able to construct a special building for its activities, funded entirely by income from its courses and programmes. It includes some sixteen classrooms, a computerized language lab, and sufficient office space for all the staff of Continuing Studies.

Another building constructed through external funding was the Technology Enterprise Facility, built through a partnership with Discovery Parks, the operating arm of the Discovery Foundation, a non-profit organization supporting high-tech development in British Columbia. It was a physical manifestation of the success of UVic's Innovation and Development Corporation.

Early in the decade, a $12 million medical building was constructed for the Island Medical Program and the Division of Medical Sciences. In 2001, UVic had reached an agreement with the UBC Medical School to accept annually twenty-four medical students (soon increased to thirty-two), students who were particularly interested in serving smaller and more remote places in BC. Because of its historic association with such communities,

UVic was well placed to undertake this initiative. UVic also possessed important supporting health science programmes in departments and centres, including Nursing, Social Work, Psychology, Health Information Sciences, Aging, Addictions Research, and Biomedical Research. Its community standing helped enlist over 600 doctors to assist with the training of the students. The first students arrived in January 2005.

In 2008, the university opened the Bob Wright Centre, Ocean, Earth, and Atmospheric Sciences Building, named for one of the university's most generous benefactors. The chief occupants of the building were the School of Earth and Ocean Sciences and the Canadian Centre for Climate Modelling and Analysis. It featured state-of-the-art classrooms, excellent communication systems, and science facilities for chemists and biologists involved in ocean research.

In the same year, the new Social Sciences and Mathematics Building, the most obviously environmentally friendly building on campus, was opened. It boasted green roofs, the use of grey water for watering greenery, energy efficient lighting, natural vegetation, and recycled building materials. It was also striking because it was grey, a marked contrast to the oranges, reds, browns and yellows of most other UVic buildings.

In 2003, the university, through a protracted and intense process, adopted a campus plan identifying environmentally significant natural areas for protection and restoration and committing UVic to sustainable practices in the construction of new buildings. Subsequently, water resources were used more sparingly, the use of pesticides was halted, Garry Oak meadows and Mystic Vale were protected, and native plants were re-introduced in landscaped areas. Several of the new UVic buildings were recognized for their environmental features through the Leadership in Energy and Environmental Design (LEED) Green Building Rating System. In addition, UVic promised to consult extensively with the community in the development of projects, not easily done as the university grows larger and more complex.

These environmental initiatives reflected strong feelings on campus. In 2000, Michael M'Gonigle, the first holder of the Eco-Research Chair of Environmental Law and Policy, established the Project on Ecological Governance (POLIS), which was initially affiliated with the Law Faculty. Its

Bob Wright (as portrayed by Myfanwy Pavelic), president and CEO of Oak Bay Marine Group of Companies, was awarded an honorary doctorate of laws by the University of Victoria in 2000. He is a tireless advocate for sustainable fishing and dedicated supporter of oceans and climate research.

left and facing page, above | Bicycles are a very popular way to move about at UVic, made easier by the facilities that have been provided for them.

facing page, below | One of the more vexatious and difficult public issues confronting UVic in recent years was "the rabbit problem," caused by people releasing rabbits they no longer wanted on the campus. They multiplied until there were some 3,000 of them. They posed some health risks and UVic, after much agonizing and sometimes heated discussion, decided it had to remove them. It was ultimately a sad development but it was not without humorous dimensions. The cartoon by Adrian Raeside provides one of these.
© Adrian Raeside

wide-ranging research interests included such issues as water and urban sustainability, cultural and ecological health, and preservation of property commons, and a continuous critique of the utilization of local situations, including the university. It joined others on campus in lobbying for even better environmental practices at UVic. The debates were typically passionate. The point is that perfection can never be achieved. There is a constant need to self-challenge; the key objective each year must be to improve what is done and how it is done.

The UVic campus was also transformed by changing traffic flows. The university allocated more spaces for bicycles and promoted their greater use. Bike repair depots were created so cyclists could conveniently undertake repairs. In 2003, UVic joined the Victoria Car Share Co-operative, which allowed people at UVic to lease cars at very economical rates for periods as short as one hour.

The big shift, however, took place through the increased use of buses. The university, with considerable help from students, notably Rob Fleming, negotiated an agreement with the Victoria Regional Transit System. In return for a lump sum from the university, it charged reduced rates to UVic faculty, staff, and students. Parking lots were used less; some of them were even converted to sites for new buildings.

....

PURSUING STRENGTHS

Cultivating effective research at a university comes from making many good choices over a long period of time. Most academics live multi-faceted lives. They have deep commitments to teaching, which, as an activity, tends to be open-ended: lecture/seminar/lab preparations will fill up whatever time is available – and there will often be an aching feeling that more time would have been useful. There are responsibilities associated with operating departments and, for many, the functioning of faculties and/or the university. Research is woven in and around these activities, though it is increasingly a part of teaching, especially in senior undergraduate and graduate courses. It can be tied into administrative work if a person is involved with a research centre. An

135

David Turpin (left), president, 2000–present, being invested with the Order of Canada by the Governor General of Canada, David Johnston, on 27 May 2011.

academic's varied life, though, is seamless and it should be, meaning that time is its most important dimension.

Research is also open-ended. Academics typically undertake projects lasting terms, even years. Preparing for them, especially applying for the requisite funding, is time consuming and, once undertaken, entails commitments that cannot easily be broken – and should not be. Academics are not like consultants who move quickly and easily from project to project depending upon opportunity and funding. Their research has an internal momentum that needs to be respected if the best results are to be achieved. The complexities mount whenever research involves several faculty members or units. Universities, therefore, rarely gain strong reputations for research activities undertaken over a short time frame. They usually emerge following a history of carefully planned appointments and specific resource allocations. They cannot, like an electric light, be immediately turned on – though they can, by poor or indifferent attention, be quickly turned off.

UVic's research successes of the last decade or so, therefore, have been possible because of the appointments and resource allocations made from the 1980s onward – in such areas as ocean sciences, computing, Aboriginal studies, business specialties (such as entrepreneurship and international business), cultural studies, various health issues, and the development of the arts. They helped determine what was possible after 2000.

UVic in 2000 continued to reap the benefit of twenty-five years of flexible and relatively continuous leadership, one that welcomed new initiatives, including interdisciplinary approaches. It also benefitted from the fact that relations between the administration and the rank and file of faculty were relatively calm, though to some extent tensions must always exist. The "Petch procedures" ensured a continuous flow of opinions and consultations throughout the ranks of the university. Furthermore, UVic had developed a talent for expediting the flow of people across administrative divides. The fact that many senior administrative personnel held office for significant periods of time helped create relatively permanent formal and informal channels of communication with the faculty, perhaps the most important requirement for peace and stability within a university.

The growth in research after 2000 can also be partly explained by the expansion of research support capacity within the administration. The new president in 2000, David Turpin, was himself a highly respected and committed researcher, a member of the Royal Society of Canada. He took a keen interest in the research activities on campus. The vice-president research, Martin Taylor, who assumed office in 1998, was also very well known for his research; his special interests in the social determinants of health fitted particularly well with some of UVic's emerging research interests. Previous administrators responsible for research, John Jackson and Alex McAuley,

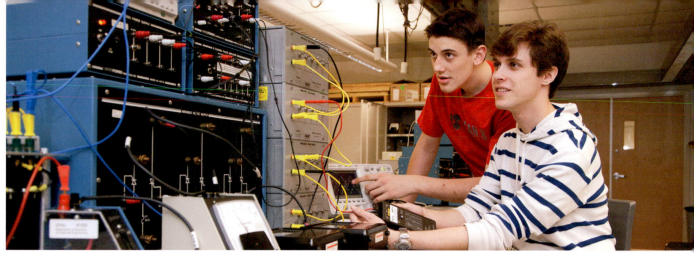

··· STUDENTS ENGAGED IN RESEARCH ···

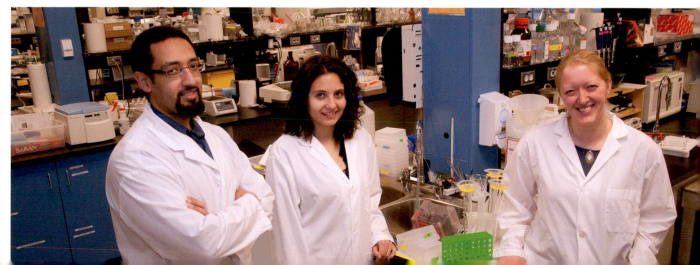

had raised the research profile considerably. In 2007, Howard Brunt became vice-president research and the research activities of the university have continued to expand under his leadership.

Much of the credit for this growth since the 1990s must also be shared by the research administrative staff, people possessing significant knowledge about various funding agencies, public and private, particularly important for UVic. UVic's remarkable research growth has emanated from a fortuitous blending of positive circumstances and committed people.

UVic was also fortunate in that federal and ultimately provincial government research priorities fitted its researchers well. In 1997, the federal government created the Canada Foundation for Innovation (CFI) to expand the research capacity of Canadian universities and to help universities attract and retain outstanding researchers already at host institutions. UVic was remarkably successful with this programme: by 2011, it had received $109,982,891 from 152 successful applications, the second largest number earned by any BC institution. Put another way, it had earned the second highest average amount of dollars from CFI awarded per full-time faculty at any Canadian university.[13]

Most awards were for sciences, engineering, and health research, but some were in the humanities and social sciences. One example of the latter was the participation by Peter Baskerville and Eric Sager of the History Department in the Canada Century Research Infrastructure Project. It utilized census and other data sources to understand how the Canadian population had changed around the turn of the twentieth century. Another was Peter Liddell's and the Humanities Computing Centre's involvement in TAPOR (Text Analysis Portal for Research), a multi-university project to digitize rare documents and tapes. This project meant that faculty and students could access resources at home rather than having to go to such places as Oxford, Paris, and Florence – though not everyone saw that development as progress.

In 2000, the federal government also announced the Canada Research Chairs programme, developed to create 2,000 research professorships across Canada. The programme helped universities fund such appointments and gave recipients grants assistance for their research costs. Over the years UVic has qualified for some thirty-five chairs (with more to come). A dozen of them were directly concerned with health research or had significant health dimensions. They contributed significantly to the expansion of UVic health research that had begun earlier. Five chairs studied environmental issues, notably some associated with oceans and climate. Two explored Aboriginal studies, and two were in mathematics. Five, notably in the Faculty of Engineering, specifically focused on computing but, in fact, nearly all of the chairs were heavily dependent on computer-based research, a bias in how the concept of "innovation" tended to be understood perhaps, but equally an indication of how important had become the manipulation of massive amounts of data.

Several chairs were awarded to initiatives not related to UVic's big projects. They included appointments in modern art, observational cosmology, theories of technology and culture, the thought of Aristotle, humanities computing, and law and society. All of them, though, regardless of the accomplishments of the individuals involved, reflected long-standing interests of people at UVic.

These programmes, along with increasing allocations by the provincial government for some specific projects, meant that UVic could build on the diverse research strengths developed over the preceding two decades. One of those areas was oceans research. The work on oceans done by earlier researchers, such as George Mackie (whose work on marine invertebrates was widely recognized and honoured by NSERC), particularly bore fruit in late 2003. As the Pacific Ocean delivered a heavy rain, Chris Barnes and various dignitaries stood on the deck of the Coast Guard ship *John P. Tully*. They had gathered to announce a $62.4 million grant from the Canadian and BC governments for the construction of NEPTUNE Canada (the North East Pacific Time-Series Undersea Networked Experiments). It was for the Canadian portion of what was to have been a partnership with the United States, a partnership that did not occur because the American side was unable to raise their funding in a timely fashion.

The NEPTUNE grant was the largest in UVic's history to that point and it was for the laying of an 800-kilometre network of fibre optic cable on the seabed off the BC coast.[14] It made possible the deposit of "laboratories" or nodes on the ocean floor about every 100 kilometres along the network. Once operational, they would provide a steady stream of data to UVic and researchers everywhere about what was happening at the bottom of the ocean. Information would become available on a part of the world where previously only passing and often fuzzy glimpses had been possible.

UVic began its continuous undersea exploration three years later, in 2006, when it launched VENUS (Victoria Experimental Network Under the Sea), which explored the waters of the Saanich Inlet and subsequently the Strait of

An underwater laboratory ready to be deposited onto the ocean floor.

Andrew Weaver, a climatologist, one of UVic's most distinguished scientists, an authority on climate change.

Georgia through its underwater cable system. It became the world leader in seafloor observatory work. NEPTUNE became operational in 2009, replacing VENUS as the world leader. The data flowing from the two networks was then distributed to scientists around the world, influencing a wide range of scientific and policy discussions and projects. The information was also organized to inform the public about the project, including videos, photographs, and websites, delivered in ways that could be particularly useful to teachers at all educational levels. The public face of the project was remarkable and can easily be found on the web.[15] In 2011, it was judged by *Popular Science* to be one of the "Universe's Ten Most Epic Projects."[16]

The expanding work on the oceans was complemented by a growth in climate studies. This interest developed in several departments and involved several researchers, but Andrew Weaver, a former UVic student who returned to the campus in 1992, played a particularly key role. His work explored how oceans affect climate, especially over long time frames. While much of his early research was on the Atlantic Ocean, its obvious applications to the Pacific Ocean were of particular interest to UVic. In fact, Weaver's reach became increasingly global in perspective as he worked on the development of global ocean climate models within the Climate Research Network (CRN). It had been established in 1993 by the Meteorological Service of Canada as part of Canada's involvement in the World Climate Program on Climate Change.

In 1995, UVic, through its Canadian Institute for Climate Studies (housed in UVic's Centre for Global Studies), assumed co-ordination of CRN, an important step in demonstrating UVic's capacity to lead complex scientific projects. In 2004, Weaver successfully applied for $3.35 million to develop a regional supercomputer to undertake advanced studies on climatic change over the last 135,000 years, looking particularly at how it affected human evolution. These accomplishments and others by climate scientists affiliated with UVic meant that in 2004 seven of them participated in the United Nations Intergovernmental Panel on Climate Change (IPCC).[17] Their work, along with that of others at UVic, contributed significantly to the Nobel Peace Prize awarded jointly to IPCC and Al Gore in 2007.

In 2005, as CRN was winding down, several on the UVic campus began working on plans to create a successor organization. Then, in February 2007, the BC government's throne speech pledged considerable funding for addressing global warming issues.[18] David Turpin, hearing of the promise, suggested to the government that it turn to the province's universities. His idea was positively received, and the dean of Science at the time, Tom Pedersen, hastily prepared a proposal. From it, and after much consultation, the Pacific Institute for Climate Solutions (PICS) was born in 2008.[19] It involved the four major BC research universities and an advisory board drawn from government, the private sector, and universities. It was (and is) charged with finding ways to reduce human impact on the climate through innovative enterprises and green technologies. It was also asked to promote greener lifestyles.

PICS received a grant for over $94 million, $90 million of it to be used to generate about $3 million each year for research into climate issues. This was the largest single contribution to a university endowment in Canada's history. PICS ultimately developed five theme areas for much of its work – building a low carbon emissions economy, social mobilization, sustainable communities, the management of carbon in BC forests, and resilient ecosystems – each profoundly important for the province's (and Canada's) future.[20] Another $1 million from the endowment would annually support the work of the Pacific Climate Impacts Consortium, also located at UVic. It developed as a non-profit corporation providing regional climatic information to various academic, governmental, and corporate stakeholders in BC and the Yukon.

People at UVic also explored energy issues. The Institute for Integrated Energy Systems (established in 1989 by David Scott) took a "big picture" approach to sustainable energy research involving engineers, economists, and environmental scientists. It became one of Canada's leading centres for research into hydrogen energy and the development of fuel cells. In 2010, a new facility, devoted to "green vehicle research" was opened, funded largely by Western Diversification Canada. Its purpose was to assist engineering faculty and students, as well as groups in the public and private sectors, to test and fine-tune the design of green vehicles powered by hybrid and electric engines. Though not everyone on campus agreed with the environmental emphasis,[21] UVic developed a remarkably large and successful commitment to environmental research.

During the 1990s, within and without the academy, more people became aware of genome research and its remarkable potential for understanding the human condition. Ben Koop, the Canada Research Chair in Genomics and Molecular Biology, was co-leader of a very large project analyzing the genes of the salmonid family of fish (salmon, trout, char, whitefish, and graylings). It explored what each gene did, thereby helping understand how fish respond to environmental change, both in the wild and in fish farms.

As the genome research grew, UVic, building on work done over the years in Biology and other departments, expanded its research into proteomics, the study of proteins. Proteomics explores the cellular make-up – the enzymes, antibodies, and molecules – of cells in living organisms, from human beings to fish to trees. It relies very much on mass spectrometry, which vaporizes atoms, turning them into ions, which are then sorted according to their masses by external electric and magnetic fields. Through a

Alan Astbury (far left) discusses research findings with colleagues, 1983.

complex process, scientists can then "fingerprint" compounds, including, for example, pesticide residues and other kinds of pollutants in cells, useful, for example, in identifying the origins and nature of street drugs and exposing steroid use among athletes. It can provide valuable assistance for improving diagnostic tests for diseases, particularly cancer, understanding the growth rates of plants, and monitoring what is happening to fish stocks. Much like the exploration of space, the seas, and genomes, it represents path-breaking ways to understand many aspects of life that previously had been mysteries at which one could only guess.

The UVic-Genome British Columbia Proteomics Centre expanded as the new century opened. It received some $7 million, much of it from governments, to develop its technical capacities and it was moved from UVic and located at the Vancouver Island Technology Park owned by UVic. Its ties to UVic nevertheless remained (and remain) close and its research activities provide analytical services to more than 200 academic, industrial, and government laboratories on a fee-for-service basis. It is particularly concerned with the medical dimensions of proteomic research, the specialty of its director, Christoph Borchers, and others associated with the centre.

Another research strength that was extended focused on forests. Dan Smith from the Geography Department worked with students and colleagues at other universities on analyzing tree rings, their size and shape, in order to understand the long-term climatic history of British Columbia and the Yukon. In 2002, UVic opened the Bev Glover Greenhouse Facility, named for a much-admired senior lab instructor. It allowed UVic forestry researchers, notably Barbara Hawkins and Peter Constabel, to work with the forestry industry and forestry communities on, for example, finding better ways to seed forests and to ensure their development. Olaf Niemann, also from Geography, carried on with similar work; in 2003–04, with the help of Western Diversification, he started the BC Centre for Applied Remote Sensing, Modelling and Simulation (BC-CARMS). It is a research resource centre that uses a variety of remote sensing techniques to understand what is happening in BC forests. The information it gathers advances research but it also greatly helps governments and private companies better manage the province's forest reserves.

The established departments also flourished. UVic's Physics Department, which is arguably the foremost example of departmental development, is a prime example of how remarkable was the growth of departmental activities. It continued its work with TRIUMF at UBC, with CERN in Switzerland, and with astronomers at the Dominion Astrophysical Observatory in Saanich. Its work in particle physics is especially noteworthy. From its beginning in the early 1980s through the work of Alan Astbury and Richard

Keeler, the particle physics group has become involved in a remarkable range of projects. Astbury played a major role at TRIUMF. His work on electromagnetism and the "weak" nuclear force contributed significantly to the team that helped the Italian Carlo Rubbia win the 1984 Nobel Prize for Physics. Astbury himself became president of the International Union of Pure and Applied Physics between 2005 and 2008. It is the most important international organization for physicists.

In recent years, younger faculty members, such as Michel Lefebvre, have become involved in major international research programmes. One of them is the ATLAS project, a national, multi-university project that explores "the laws of nature, and the very fabric of space-time, at the smallest distance scale ever."[22] Working with a detector the "size of a seven story apartment building," Lefebvre and his colleagues are able to "'see' down to scales 50,000 times smaller than a proton, which is itself about 10,000 times smaller than an atom, which is itself about 5,000 times smaller than the wavelength of visible light, which is the smallest size one can see with a conventional optical microscope (about 1 micrometre, or a thousandth of a millimetre)."[23] It is part of one of the most exciting frontiers engaging the human mind today. When asked by the author to suggest what the questions on this frontier were, Lefebvre wrote:

- What is the origin of mass?
- What is the nature of Dark Matter?
- Why is there more matter than anti-matter in the visible universe?
- Can all known forces be unified?
- Are there other spatial dimensions?
- Are fundamental particles really fundamental?
- And many others![24]

In addition, the particle physics group is involved with a number of other important international projects; BaBar, which explores matter-antimatter asymmetry in nature; T2K, a multinational particle physics project exploring muon neutrinos, one of nature's basic particles; and the Thirty-Metre Telescope, a new optical telescope being developed near Pasadena. It is difficult to decide which of these initiatives is

A new 0.8 metre DFM telescope was installed in July 2010. UVic students can now explore the observable universe with the largest on-campus telescope in Canada. (Photo: Darren Stone)

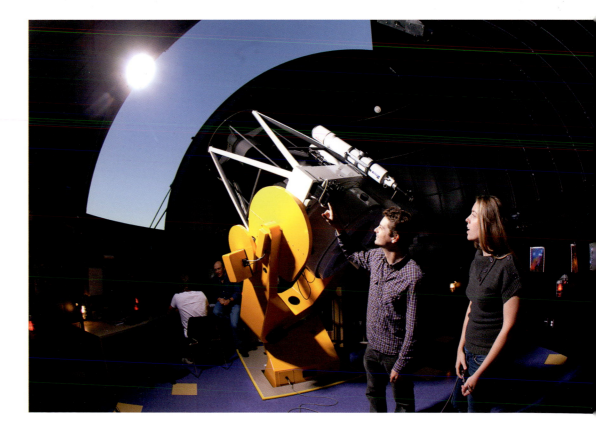

Vancouver Island Technology Park

the more difficult to comprehend – the ones addressing the infinities of space or those examining the complexities of matter to a level the imagination strains to understand.

The successes of these and other forms of research at UVic, as well as the success of the UVic Innovation and Development Corporation (after 2011, UVic Industry Partnerships), led UVic to develop a technology park as a way of expanding university connections with governments and business. It was acquired in 2005, largely through the efforts of David Turpin, and organized as a business financially separate from UVic and operated by an independent board, a structure not unlike that of crown corporations. By 2011, UVic's Vancouver Island Technology Park was hosting twenty-three companies, employing 1,300 people, and contributing over $280 million to the BC economy. The companies were concentrated in the information and communication industries, particularly in media, life science, clean-tech, and ocean tech fields.

....

THE DIVERSITIES OF INTEREST

Much of the publicity, much of the special funding, for research, for new ways of learning, at UVic was devoted to science and engineering, perhaps understandable because those were the more favoured areas for government research support. The research in other parts of the university, however, while less prominent and without the very large financial dimensions, was nevertheless important. Much of it was directed at the social and economic problems within society. That focus was not without controversy since, stated rather simplistically, there is a continuum of views on what is appropriate.

At one end of the continuum are those who argue that universities in their teaching and research should only be concerned with the kind of research that grows out of established, provable, replicable, and permanent research – the kind of knowledge historically (if simplistically) associated with science and what can be called the scientific method. It sees knowledge as being built incrementally, explored hypotheses contributing as they can to recognizable theory, until sound and expandable understandings, approximating (maybe even achieving) truth, is achieved.

··· STUDENTS ON CO-OP WORK TERMS ···

At the other end of the polarity are those who argue that universities must be "involved in the world," addressing key and complex contemporary issues and trying to help resolve them either through providing service as asked or by becoming active agents in fostering change. The latter approach starts with contemporary issues and changing ways of viewing and responding to them. It does not so much create final conclusions about issues, their identity and resolution, as it offers alternative ways to understand and to affect them. It begs, borrows, and incorporates methods from a wide menu, producing results that advance understandings and encourage social action. It raises awkward questions about how researchers, whatever their good intentions, undertake their work. It tends, almost invariably, to suggest the need for more research rather than arriving at definitive conclusions. It questions whether final or absolute truth – or any approximation of it – is ever possible.

There have always been debates within the academy about such issues, especially by those inhabiting the two polarities, but they became particularly pronounced in the twenty years after 1990, when UVic became increasingly involved in many broad kinds of inquiry.[25] As the years went by, UVic tended to accept forms of socially engaged research (albeit as organized through the federal government's funding councils), but the debate continued and it continues; realistically, it will never end. The extremes of the two sides, as one might expect, have seldom found comfortable room for accommodation. Ultimately, though some might disagree, it is a debate that should aim to be a healthy dialogue, conducted in an open, thoughtful, and respectful way. It is in so doing that the best "truth" we can achieve at any given time can be gained.

....

REACHING OUTWARD

From 2000 onward UVic expanded its commitment to experiential learning. The co-op programme continued to prosper (serving about 2,700 each year) and UVic remained Western Canada's leading practitioner of this kind of learning. The Faculty of Human and Social Development, particularly through its schools of Nursing and Health Information Science, developed an international reputation[26] – and much local appreciation – for its efforts in engaging locally-based training programmes for health professionals, many of them through online systems. The Law Faculty's Law Centre clinical term, and its Environmental Law Centre, provided increasingly appreciated services to many individuals and groups within British Columbia, especially the nearby communities. Experiential learning was fundamental

to the community-based research activities that became prominent at UVic during the first years of the twenty-first century.

In fact, UVic's growing commitment to serving communities, near and far, had become a central focus of its institutional life. This is apparent in some of the larger projects discussed above; it is also obvious in the work of some of the individual researchers who have made several important contributions to local communities. A few examples from many make the case.

- Asit Mazumder, an aquatic ecologist and Natural Sciences and Engineering Research Council Industrial Research Chair at UVic, worked closely with the Capital Regional District and other local BC governments in evaluating and better managing their water resources. This work took him, his colleagues, and students elsewhere in BC and Central Canada to help develop secure water supplies for Canadian communities, unfortunately a matter of growing concern.

left | Asit Mazumder, holder of a Natural Sciences and Engineering Research Council Chair in Water whose work addresses some of the growing problems associated with water locally, regionally, nationally, and internationally. Photo: Diana Nethercott.

right | Tłı̨chǫ Dictionary Research Workshop, Edzo, NWT, November 2010.

CanAssist was started by Nigel Livingston, from the Biology Department, as a volunteer effort to see how the capacities of the university, particularly technology, can be mobilized to assist people with disabilities. Today it has a core team of professionals drawn from several departments at UVic and the community, and it offers a range of programmes to help people with different disabilities. Students play a major role in its activities, as volunteers or co-op students, as researchers, or as part of an academic programme. It is one of the happiest places on the UVic campus.

- Bonnie Leadbeater from the Department of Psychology, and with support from the Rock Solid Foundation, helped local schools deal with student bullying.
- Leslie Saxon (Linguistics) worked with researchers and educators in the Tłı̨chǫ communities between Great Slave Lake and Great Bear Lake to prepare place names reports, Tłı̨chǫ dictionaries in three formats, a Tłı̨chǫ literacy manual, and story books and curriculum plans supporting language and culture education in Tłı̨chǫ schools and homes through UVic's Certificate Program in Aboriginal Language Revitalization.
- Michael Asch (Anthropology) provided valuable insights into the role played by culture and particularly cultural difference in resolving economic and political issues in Canada.

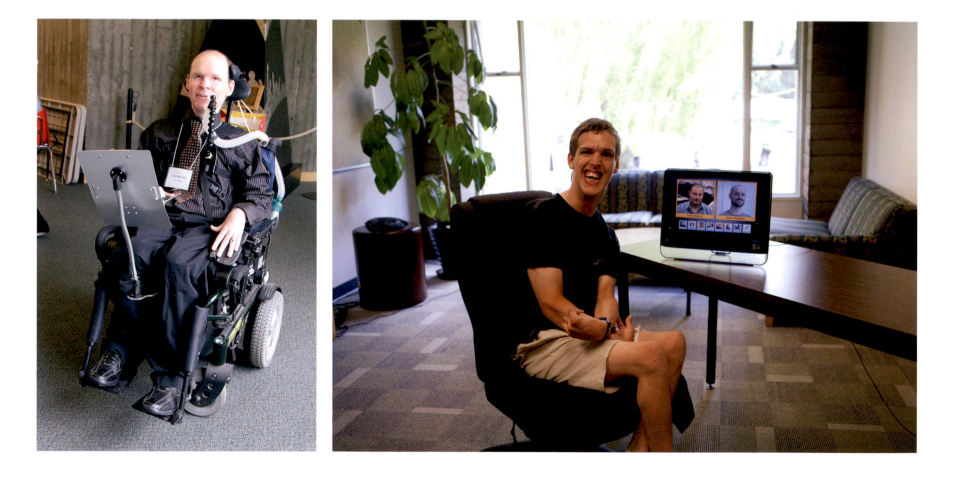

- Tim Stockwell became director of the newly created Centre for Addictions Research of British Columbia in 2004. David Turpin played a very important role in bringing this centre to UVic and in developing its financial resources. The centre has worked with other BC universities to explore such subjects as substance impaired driving, different dimensions of alcohol abuse, the development of the concepts of "helping communities" and "helping schools," guidance advice for parents of young teenagers, and the specific addiction problems of street youth and sex workers. Much of its work involves local community collaborators. Its research is aimed at international scholarly audiences and public officials in many jurisdictions.
- Members of the French Department expanded their work with l'Alliance Française and in support of francophones in British Columbia, carrying on a tradition going back to the days of Victoria College.
- Larry McCann in Geography provided a valuable model for inquiry into the nature of local communities through an extensive database on Oak Bay.
- Neena Chappell and Holly Tuokko (Centre on Aging) provided important insights into the relationships between mental health and aging.
- Marge Reitsma-Street and colleagues in the university and several community partners developed greater understanding of poverty in Victoria.
- The Faculties of Human and Social Development and Law provided contexts within which the resolution of disputes became a focus of research and teaching. Maureen Maloney, holder of the Dorothy and David Lam Chair in Law and Public Policy, made a remarkable contribution to this field of endeavour.
- Cecilia Benoit, from Sociology, and some of her students provided an extensive analysis of the sex trade in Victoria and raised questions about how it should be viewed.
- The British Columbia Institute for Co-operative Studies (2000–09) raised over $5 million to work with several local communities and co-operative organizations in an effort to develop a serious, sustained, interdisciplinary, and international academic analysis of a form of enterprise that has over one billion members around the globe, employs many more people than the multinationals, and provides at least one key service to half the world's population.
- A group of students and faculty started Humanities 101 (subsequently, University 101), a course for people who otherwise would not be at a university (some were street people). Faculty members volunteered

Many UVic students go on to have remarkable careers. For example, Tamara Vrooman, following an outstanding career in the public service, went on to become chief executive officer of Vancity Credit Union, Canada's largest credit union. Here she speaks to a class in history (she was a graduate student in that discipline at UVic) about how her university studies prepared her for her working life.

University 101 is a UVic initiative supported by individuals and organizations in the Greater Victoria area to offer free, non-credit university courses to people who have faced barriers to post-secondary education. Students attend classes twice a week to learn about a wide range of topics in the Humanities and Social Sciences from volunteer faculty at UVic. Course materials, meals, transportation, and childcare subsidies are provided. Students are active participants in the class, drawing on their knowledge and experience with the topics, as well as their enthusiasm for learning.

their time to give special lectures organized by students into coherent patterns of topics.

- Christine Welsh, with the assistance of a student, Jessica Wood, prepared a documentary, *Finding Dawn*, that explored the pressing issue of missing Aboriginal women, a topic that had gone underreported in the media and had not been given the attention it deserved in public discourse.

While many of the efforts to reach out and serve communities by helping to address specific and economic issues were focused on nearby places, the international work that had started in the previous decade continued, as a few examples will show.

- UVic's International Institute for Child Rights and Development, funded by the Canadian International Development Agency, worked with the RCMP, UNICEF, and Microsoft in the development of software that helps identify and arrest people responsible for online child exploitation.
- In 2008, African specialists came together to form a network at UVic to encourage collaboration and sponsor events concerned with African issues.
- Terry Pearson (Biochemistry and Microbiology) undertook notable research in studying parasites causing African sleeping sickness and other parasites that kill fish in different parts of the world.
- Joe Kess (Linguistics) became a Fellow of the Royal Society of Canada and a recipient of the Order of the Rising Sun from the Japanese government (the highest honour bestowed by Japan on foreign nationals), for his work in psycholinguistics, sociolinguistics, and the relationship between language, ethnicity, and the discourse of identity.
- Alan Pence (Child and Youth Care), UNESCO Chair for Early Childhood Education, Care and Development, has earned many honours for his work in Canada and other countries. In 1989, he established the First Nations Partnerships Program, working with First Nations people in Western Canada. In 1999, he founded the Early Childhood Development Virtual University, con-

centrated in Africa. It trains mid-career professionals in several countries to help them develop early childhood programmes funded by UNICEF, the World Bank, and CIDA. It follows a "generative curriculum" approach emphasizing community-based, learner-centred methodologies.

One of the most important sets of community relations came through the work of people at UVic and in communities to build Indigenous studies on campus. Student recruiters made special efforts to encourage Indigenous youth to come to UVic. Several departments revised their curriculum to include serious and sustained examination of the experience of Indigenous peoples. It took many different forms: the engagement of elders in the transmission of knowledge; working with community educators in designing curriculum that honoured Aboriginal knowledge; encouraging the development of Aboriginal businesses; helping Aboriginal women meet their challenges; understanding historically how Aboriginal people were displaced as the BC economy developed; assisting young Aboriginal people to succeed at UVic; exploring First Nations cultures; and developing social work programmes that would be useful.

This general interest on campus led to discussions about the development of a First Peoples House. Initiated by the Faculty of Human and Social Development, it soon became an institutional priority, championed by President Turpin. It entailed years of conversations with First Nations groups on southern Vancouver Island about what the building should be like and what its essential purposes should be. Its first purpose, it was decided, would be to provide a welcoming place for First Nations students, a place where they could learn about and honour their cultures and traditions. Its second purpose would be to provide a location where others could better understand Indigenous heritage and current issues, and to promote intercultural understanding.

In a sense, when the First Peoples House opened its doors in October 2009, the gathering of knowledge in Gordon Head had completed a circle. The centuries of understandings that had been preserved and handed on by Aboriginal peoples – and had been rather cruelly cast aside, even repressed by others – had returned. It had become one of

A face-to-face meeting of some of the people involved in the Early Childhood Development Virtual University at Lake Malawi (also known as Lake Nyasi), ca. 2006. Alan Pence is in the back row, far left.

··· HONOURING INDIGENOUS CULTURE ···

the most obvious and appreciated ways of knowing on campus, reflected in a remarkable building surrounded by native plants. The split between Indigenous knowledge and the structured educational systems of the Euro-Canadian world, an unfortunate fact of history, was being bridged, gradually perhaps, but purposefully.

Another reflection of the increasing interests in communities, near and far, was the emergence of an interest in community-based research. It owed much to the work of Budd Hall, an adult educator, and a group of individuals and units on campus he selected to participate in the work of the Office for Community-based Research. At the same time, interest in this approach led the School of Public Administration to develop a master's programme in Community Development and Ana Maria Peredo (Business) to develop the Centre for Co-operative and Community-Based Economy, building on the base provided by the BC Institute for Co-operative Studies. All these initiatives were devoted to broad and diverse ways in which people in communities can mobilize and harness economic and social resources.

This emphasis on community-based research is a natural development at UVic, given its historic community connections and the interests of many faculty members and students. It is not, however, an easy form of research. It requires genuine mutual exchange of knowledge between universities and communities, not unlike what has painstakingly been learned – and continues to be learned – in Indigenous studies. It is not just the transfer of knowledge from the university world, though that is how some academics tend to see it. It also requires collaborative and open relationship within the academic community, not easy since academics generally are trained – and are largely rewarded – on the basis of individual progress and recognition. Transferring that mindset unthinkingly to community-based research will blunt its possibilities. The rewards, however, both in terms of the knowledge that can be gained and the results that can be achieved more than repay the effort and rethinking that is required.

Such then are some of the major research trends at UVic in recent years. Understanding research, however, is somewhat like reviewing how people have thought about New France. It is enticing to interpret the history of that colony largely by examining the stories of the big flotillas – the groupings of sailing vessels that brought the armies, the clergy, and the settlers, that moved the goods and armaments between the St Lawrence and France. They seemed important because they were the special projects of the governments of the day. In retrospect, though, they were hardly more important than the lonely canoe paddlers who journeyed inland and, with the help of the people they found there, opened a continent. More than the flotillas, they shaped the bigger and lasting history of their colony and the nation Canadians today inhabit.

Who killed William Robinson, a black man, on nearby Salt Spring Island in 1867? Was it really the local Indigenous man who was hanged for the crime? When historians Ruth Sandwell and John Lutz put the evidence online in 1999 and invited students to re-examine the murder, they launched a project that now includes a dozen major mystery websites and another thirty more detailed ones, in French and English, that, on average, allow students to try and solve old mysteries but, even more importantly, to learn more about aspects of Canadian history not commonly considered in history courses. *The Great Unsolved Mysteries in Canadian History* is based in the History Department, and has won the Pierre Berton Prize for making Canadians interested in their history as well as the Merlot Prize for the best history on the web.

Research is like that. While UVic has been engaged in several large-scale formally and informally connected research projects, numerous individual researchers have pursued their own research topics. Their research or creative activity has enriched their teaching, attracted students, changed curricula, and intrigued people in the community through courses and public lectures. It has made some individual academics important in their disciplines and, in some instances, notable public intellectuals. A few examples, again from very many, will make the point.

- John Lutz (History) and others developed a website, *Who Killed William Robinson? Race, Justice and Settling the Land*, showing how one can understand aspects of the country's social, cultural, and economic past by examining historic crimes and how they were (or were not) dealt with.
- Joan Wharf-Higgins (Education) is an authority on community and population health and physical activity, health literacy and healthy communities, and the application of social marketing to facilitate social change.
- Hamar Foster (Law) is an expert on the legal history of the fur trade, BC legal history, and Aboriginal law.
- Brian Dippie (History) is one of the foremost interpreters of the American West, particularly western art and the saga of George Custer.
- Eike-Henner Kluge (Philosophy) is one of Canada's most consulted experts on ethical issues.
- Andrew Rippin is a distinguished Islamic scholar.
- Patricia Roy (History), one of Canada's foremost historians, examines the history of Asian peoples in British Columbia.
- John McLaren (Law), an historian of the law, is well-known for his work on the Doukhobors, BC legal history, and comparative national legal histories.
- James Tully is a very distinguished scholar in contemporary political and legal philosophy (or theory) and its history, and in Canadian political and legal philosophy.

All told, the expansion of research at UVic in recent years has been remarkable. In the 2010 Re$earch Infosource ranking of Canada's research universities, UVic topped all other

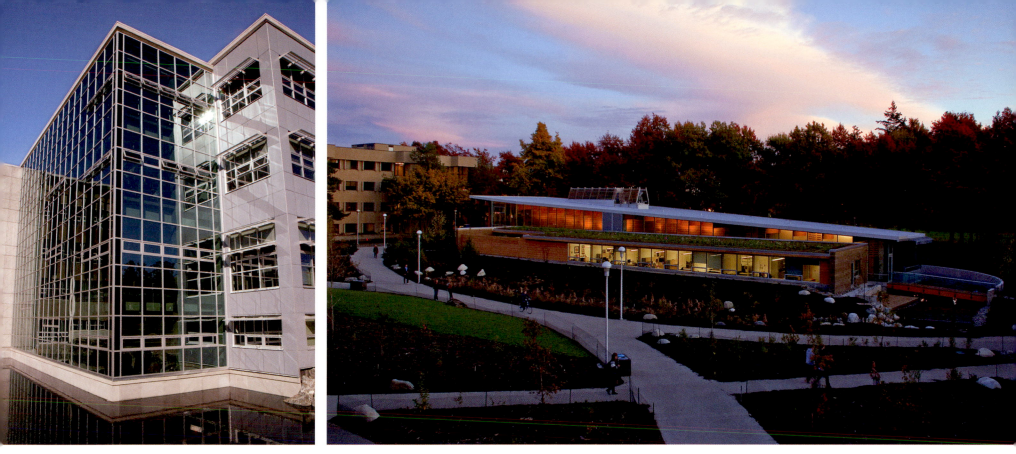

··· THE BUILDINGS AFTER 2000: THE LEGACY ···

BOB WRIGHT CENTRE
OCEAN, EARTH AND
ATMOSPHERIC SCIENCES

universities in its class in two out of three measures of research performance and growth in research intensity.[27] In the same year, it was ranked 130th in the world and held sixth place in Canada in the *Times Higher Education*'s annual World University Rankings. It was the top-ranked university in Canada without a medical school.

....

RESTRUCTURED

The growth of research should not be seen in isolation. It took place within a university that had changed rapidly and would continue to do so. In 2011, UVic taught nearly 20,000 students in its regular programmes, and had an enrolment of 16,000 in its Continuing Studies programmes; it had ten faculties, two divisions, forty departments, and fifteen centres; it housed 2,300 people in its residences; it employed over 5,000 people; its annual financial impact on the local economy totaled $3 billion; its commitment to experiential learning magnified its contributions to communities, near and far; its interest in community-based research reflected its desire to help build a better world; it owned just over 169 hectares of property at Gordon Head and another sixty hectares elsewhere on Vancouver Island (including the purchase in 2010 of the Queenswood property from the Sisters of St Ann); it had significant national and international associations with other universities, research institutes, government organizations, and private businesses; it was committed to sustaining strong teaching programmes; and it had become a significant research university. It was a large and diversified institution difficult to grasp in its totality, but significant in its impact. In the years since 2000 it had captured significantly more of the reputation it had earned through a remarkable expansion in what it did; it had sustained a commendable effort to preserve pursuit of what was ultimately really important.

In the process, the contours of the university had changed. The creation of spin-off organizations had altered the institutional structure, the impact of which only time will tell. The arrival of Big Science – for example, that associated with the oceans and climate – altered relationships with governments, communities, and businesses; it created new and powerful networks on campus. The expanding impact of computers multiplied the information from which knowledge could be derived. The makeup of the campus – students, staff, and faculty – was profoundly different from what it had been. The relationships with communities had evolved. Administrative structures concerned with enhanced advocacy capacity on behalf of UVic and universities generally had been substantially enhanced. Planning, which had in earlier years been important but hardly central, had become integral to how the university functioned, it seemed on a daily basis. Teaching and learning, which had changed little over decades, seemed on the cusp of an extensive reformulation. Actions were becoming steadily more methodical, procedures more important; UVic had developed a remarkably comprehensive set of manuals and regulations. Routine tasks were increasingly added to local departments, transforming the distribution of administrative work on campus. The university strove to become more accountable, not easy as it grew quickly. It struggled to keep communication systems open, to retain, even enhance, the sense of community that had generally prevailed at UVic over the years. It worked hard on its brand, on co-ordination, and cohesion. Increased size, change, and diversity brought their rewards; they also brought their challenges; UVic had been transformed in the first decade of the new century.

right | Michael Williams was an English immigrant who became involved in heritage reconstruction in Victoria. He was a generous benefactor of his adopted community and of the University of Victoria. He was a collector of the art of the West Coast, particularly that of the First Nations peoples. When he passed away in 2000, he willed a large donation to UVic. Part of that donation has been used to develop the Legacy Gallery in the centre of the city. It houses his collections and those of the university.

overleaf | Aerial view, 2010

··· FLOWERS OF UVIC ···

9

....

BALANCING

UVic has changed remarkably in fifty years. So too have Canadian universities generally, especially recently. Since 1995 undergraduate enrolments in Canada's post-secondary institutions have nearly doubled, reaching some 870,000 (733,000 undergraduate, 136,000 graduate). Government support for university operating costs has more than doubled, from $5.4 billion to $11.1 billion. The number of faculty has increased by some 6,000 to 40,000. Federal government research funding (from which UVic has particularly benefitted) has grown from $1.2 billion to $4.2 billion.[1]

UVic growth and development, therefore, while largely because of what people involved with it have chosen to do and have been able to do well, has also owed much to favourable circumstances: students have come – and continue to come – in growing numbers; governments, federal and provincial, have generally been more supportive as their commitments to what they call the "knowledge economy" increase in importance; and reciprocal relationships with communities, near and far, have steadily deepened to UVic's great benefit.

These generally favourable situations may continue. They may not. Regardless of what the future may bring, though, what patterns from UVic's past might be useful for dealing with the future, whatever its course?

When universities started to emerge in Europe some 700 to 800 years ago, one of their objectives came to be reaching out across the ages to the wisdom of the Ancients – Aristotle, Plato, and many others. One of the reasons many classical thinkers appealed was that running through their ideas (but particularly the work of Aristotle) was a search for balance, in fact, the balanced life. That goal still attracts and perhaps it can provide as useful a guide as any in reflecting on what is important to keep in mind about UVic's heritage and situation.

Universities are always subject to myriad pressures, some coming from within – the restless and relentless pressures from scholars will always create demands. Others come from without – the world does not stand idly by and many scholars are deeply engaged in the life around them. Universities, therefore, must constantly make choices in response to these pressures, but the choices are rarely "either/or." They are choices along continua; choices between two contrasting polarities, or more likely, choices blending essential points from both, typically complex balancing acts.

Some continua have been abundantly obvious in the history of UVic, the search for balance within them being a way to make sense of much of its history.

....

TEACHING/RESEARCH

UVic started as a university with deep commitments to teaching, in keeping with the Liberal Arts tradition. Amid the tensions and changes of the 1960s and 1970s, the balance shifted towards research, affecting appointments, curriculum, and structures. Lately, the balance has been shifting back to the middle, as it becomes more obvious that the connections between research and teaching are as important as the tensions. In the process, many of the values of Liberal Arts – for informed and rigorous opinions, for a broad humanistic view of life, and for quests beyond ritualized thought – have reasserted themselves; values that have been qualified from their historical meaning by several critiques based on gender analysis, cultural awareness, and critical thinking.

Moreover, it has become increasingly clear that if teaching suffers, so ultimately does research – and vice versa. Research takes many different forms and is found in many places. It is undertaken by many different kinds of people. Learning flows in many directions. What that means for how universities discover, organize, and transmit thought is one of the great challenges they face; finding and sustaining the right balance will not be easily done at UVic or anywhere else.

....

SKILLS/REFLECTION

From the 1970s onward, UVic has been engaged in the development of pro-fessional schools and various programmes. Their development has incited considerable controversies, largely because some faculty members have feared they would lead more to training than education, that the univer-sity's main purposes would be lost. This perspective undervalues the kind of self-analysis carried on by people engaged in professional/vocational programmes. It also denies discussions that do belong at a university as well as elsewhere.

We live in a world where errors beyond calculation have been made with what we have chosen to do and how we have chosen to do it; by how little we have considered the ramifications of how we organize; the ethical beliefs we apply (or don't) in our daily activities; and the faulty relationships we create. Those errors have as much to do with our workplaces as with anywhere else.

There should be space at universities to reflect on them and that should not happen in isolation, removed from practice. There should be opportunities for discussions of the appropriateness and consequences of the kinds of work we do, discussions that range across several disciplines and engage diverse perspectives. Where training ends and education begins, after all, is not a simple matter, but it needs to be thought about. The continuum, which easily is lost through casual assumptions or immediate gain, is one that always needs to be emphasized at a university.

INFORMATION/SYNTHESIS

The amount of information directed at people today surpasses comprehension. Continuous sound bites and scattered pieces of information can create the illusion of understanding. Mastering the latest communication innovation can easily trick people into thinking they have mastered content. The struggle to keep up with technical innovation can overwhelm the need to digest and to synthesize.

On the one hand, as UVic has demonstrated in so many ways, universities must strive to access the information revolutions sweeping our world. They must create spaces, such as that found in the Mearns Centre, where information flows easily and people can be irresistibly engaged. On the other, they must strive for the harder part: to make sense of it all. It is not an easy task. The synthesis polarity of the continuum has rarely been mastered; the human capacity to blend well what scientists and poets, philosophers and business specialists, religious scholars and physicists have produced has not been very impressive. The news each night tells the tale. The disciplinary boundaries that have been created to organize thought have too often advanced flawed paradigms. Universities should be places where such efforts at synthesis can be more deeply pursued, as difficult and uncomfortable as doing so might be.

DETACHMENT/ENGAGEMENT

The mainstream inherited tradition of the university world emphasizes detachment, envisions places where the pressures of the world do not limit enquiry, where it is possible to pursue thought for its own sake, and where reflection occurs at its appropriate pace. There is a kind of logic to this perspective, for the search for knowledge demands time for quiet concentration, a rare gift in the modern world. Universities, therefore, can contribute an inestimable social benefit by providing it for students and scholars.

One of UVic's oldest, continuing international associations has been with East China Normal University (ECNU). Pictured above, UVic President David Turpin and his wife, Suromitra Sanatani, are guests of honour at the ECNU International Culture Festival Gala celebrating ECNU's sixtieth anniversary and the thirtieth anniversary of the ECNU–UVic partnership, Shanghai, 16 October 2011. Second from the left: ECNU President Yu Lizhong. (Photo: Elsa Yan)

On the other hand, universities can never be completely aloof from the communities in which they exist and that they serve; nor should they try in all ways to be. Much of the knowledge they impart is gathered in reciprocal and mutual relationships with outsiders: Indigenous communities, professional associations, working people, governments, economic organizations, civil society, ethnic communities, and population groups defined by geography, class, gender, or other forms of differentiation and bonds of association. Nor is the information gathered always comfortable to consider: the university as critic is an historic and valuable role, one that should raise questions not easily raised by others. This is a continuum of immense importance to UVic, given its growing work in and with communities. Finding the right balance will be crucial for its future.

LOCAL/GLOBAL

In recent years, UVic has undertaken a highly commendable effort to internationalize its curriculum, a necessary commitment as the world shrinks, as the global economy changes, and as the need for deepened cultural understandings becomes painfully obvious. At the same time, UVic is drawn more into local developments and local issues. How should the balance be made – in how enrolments are managed, research agendas decided, curriculum developed? Are local and global opposite sides of the same coin? Are the issues facing one also facing the other but perhaps defined in different ways? Or is that a naïve faith?

UTILITY/BEAUTY

As student numbers grow and the campus adjusts to their demands, as universities are enlisted consciously in economic development, it is easy to pass over the fact that universities are also custodians of beauty. In UVic those who have been responsible for its grounds have borne much of that responsibility and they have done so well. There are, however, other contributions, most obviously in the public art, especially that of Indigenous peoples, the gifts bestowed by the University of Victoria Art Collections, the work of the artists associated with the Faculty of Fine Arts, the displays in the library, and more recently the exhibits of the Legacy Gallery downtown. Thought of another way, beauty is also preserved and enhanced by the music, theatre, and poetry one readily finds on campus and, indeed, in the rhythms of the languages that are taught. How does one balance the utilitarian imperative with the artistic and cultural responsibilities – the demands of "Big Science" and professional schools with the needs of artists, poets, philosophers? How does one highlight best the insights of a multiplicity of cultures? It is not easy to establish such balances. It is not easy to find the courage to defend them.

....

PLANS AND FLEXIBILITY

The last decade in particular has ushered in a remarkable commitment to planning, carefully developed and conscientiously applied. The benefits have been enormous: it is one of the reasons why UVic has been able to project clearer messages about itself, compete more effectively for substantial research grants, attack some of the major problems of our time, and commit resources more easily. Plans can, however, becomes traps; logical procedures obstacles; the resultant hierarchies barriers to communications. That has not happened yet at UVic. Much of the flexibility and creativity that began to blossom in the late 1970s, that spilled across the campus and was nurtured by faculty members and administrators, remains. The challenge will be to sustain them.

In order that the best choices on the continua be made, it is also important that people at UVic continue to strive for harmony, avoiding the hubris of extolling one's own way of knowing over others, and striving to be steadily more inclusive. The purpose of a university is not to create academic "stars" or to build individual careers; it is about many people engaging the worlds of ideas, beliefs, and sentiments; of exploring the limits of space, the depth of oceans, the past and present of cultures, the immense creativity of the human spirit, the varieties of communities. It is necessarily about creating the kind of community that can do these things well and in several directions at the same time.

At the end, universities are places of privilege but not because historically they have tended to be places for the economically and socially privileged. They are privileged because they are places that aspire to free enquiry, places of the mind where clarity of thought, effectiveness of communication, and tolerance of difference can be appreciated and pursued. They are also places where the value of intuition, imagination, and sentiment – sometimes even the sentimental – can be useful alongside approaches that are rigorously systematic. Such places take on added value in an age of information overload and engulfing, demeaning consumerism. They can provide an important antidote to the disappointments, excessive careerism, narcissism, and petty rivalries that life can bring, even in student days and especially afterwards. Once genuinely begun, the quest cannot be snuffed out. That is as true of UVic as anywhere else.

Those who work at universities – in the registrar's office, student services, the cafeterias, the grounds, human resources, the residences, the accountants' offices, the departmental, faculty, and institute offices, as well as in classrooms – can readily see around them the special qualities of university life: for example, how special is the time students spend on campus. On any given day, it is not difficult to see them engaging in the kinds of reflection that the busyness of later years may tend to crowd out; learning how to balance the intellectual, social, and physical dimensions of their lives; and discussing the issues today that must necessarily be considered if they are to live the examined life.

And what is it that is special about the way UVic tries to conduct its affairs? David Turpin is fond of saying that UVic is well-suited to the contemporary challenges of university life because of its size, which he characterizes as "big enough to do big things, small enough to get to know each other, and small enough not to think we can do it all by ourselves. It's good to be humble, it's good to collaborate."[2] It is a quintessentially UVic statement. It suggests that dreams beckon, that flexibility is important, that humility before the enormity of what is to be done is preferable to arrogance, and that collaboration is necessary for success. It is a good summary of what UVic, at its best, has tried to be.

··· STUDENT LIFE AT UVIC ···

APPENDICES

APPENDIX 1: A WORD ON SOURCES

Because of its comparative brevity and primary purposes, this historical essay is based on only a small portion of the massive documentation concerning the University of Victoria housed within the UVic Archives. Generally, in searching through the archives I primarily consulted those documents that examined the overall patterns of the university's development. I was looking for the general trends of UVic's history rather than trying to develop a detailed grasp of the many issues that crowd its past and present.

I relied heavily on the work of Peter Smith, (*A Multitude of the Wise: UVic Remembered* [Victoria: The Alumni Association of the University of Victoria, 1993]) and Edward B. Harvey (ed., *The Lansdowne Era: Victoria College, 1946–1963* [Montreal and Kingston: McGill-Queen's University Press, 2008]) in providing an overview of the main trends within the history of Victoria College. In understanding the development of more recent years, I used reports in *The Ring*, the university's main publication, frequently and, to a lesser extent, *The Martlet*, the main student publication. I consulted such departmental and unit histories as have been prepared, and they have been referenced in the footnotes. I hope this publication will encourage more units on campus to prepare such histories.

This book is not intended as a full history of the institution. That much greater (and I am sure very rewarding) task still awaits its historian. Rather, it is primarily a personal distillation of a series of recorded conversations with over 160 colleagues at the university. Copies of those conversations will be placed in the UVic Archives late in 2012. I also relied heavily on my own involvement at UVic since 1976, which included periods on secondment to Extension Services and as chair of the Department of History (1982–89), dean of Humanities (1992–99), and director of the British Columbia Institute for Co-operative Studies (2000–08).

In my conversations with colleagues, I tried repeatedly to check my understandings of what happened with theirs in order to ferret out my mistaken views. To my chagrin, I found out that there were far more of those than I would have previously admitted. Above all, though, the interviews gave me the opportunity to grasp how diverse, complex, and remarkable is a university like UVic. I hope I have accurately and fairly captured at least some of their understandings and reflections in this essay.

Ian MacPherson
December 2011

....

APPENDIX 2: THE CHANCELLORS

1963–66	Joseph B. Clearihue
1967–69	Richard B. Wilson
1970–72	Roderick L. Haig-Brown
1973–78	Robert T.D. Wallace
1979–84	Ian McTaggart-Cowan
1985–90	William C. Gibson
1991–96	Hon. Robert G. Rogers
1997–2002	Norma Mickelson
2003–08	Ronald Lou-Poy
2009–present	Murray Farmer

....

APPENDIX 3: THE PRESIDENT AND VICE-CHANCELLORS

1963–64	W. Harry Hickman*
1964–68	Malcolm G. Taylor
1968–69	Robert T.D. Wallace*
1969–72	Bruce J. Partridge
1972–74	Hugh E. Farquhar
1974	Stephen A. Jennings*
1975–90	Howard E. Petch
1990–2000	David F. Strong
2000–present	David H. Turpin

* Acting president

APPENDIX 4: THE CHAIRS OF THE BOARD OF GOVERNORS

(Prior to 1999, "chairmen")

1963–66	Joseph B. Clearihue
1967–69	Richard B. Wilson
1969–71	Willard E. Ireland
1971–72	Lloyd G. McKenzie
1972–73	David Angus
1973–79	S. Joseph Cunliffe
1979–82	Hugh R. Stephen
1982–85	Ian H. Stewart
1985–87	George P. Kidd
1987–92	Ian H. Stewart
1992–93	Douglas J. Enns
1993–94	David S. Philip
1994–97	Sandra J. Harper
1997–2000	Brian J. Lamb
2000–01	Roger Wheelock
2001–03	Linda Dryden
2003–05	Eric Donald
2005–07	Trudi Brown
2007–08	Murray Farmer
2008–10	Ray Protti
2010–present	Susan Mehinagic

APPENDIX 5: PRESIDENTS OF THE FACULTY ASSOCIATION

1963–64	Geoffrey P. Mason
1964–65	Roy E.L. Watson
1965–66	Peter L. Smith
1966–67	David J. Chabassol
1967–68	Izzud-Din Pal
1968–69	James E. Hendrickson
1969–70	Leo I. Bakony
1970–71	Donald Harvey
1971–72	Charles Doyle

1972–73	John C.E. Greene
1973–74	John A. Downing
1974–75	Charles W. Tolman
1975–76	David F. Henn
1976–77	Rodney T.K. Symington
1977–78	J. Anthony Burke
1978–79	Richard J. Powers
1979–80	Samuel E. Scully
1980–81	Trevor L. Williams
1981–82	Gerald A. Poulton
1982–84	Gordon S. Shrimpton
1984–85	William E. Pfaffenberger
1985–86	Larry D. Yore
1986–87	Roy E.L. Watson
1987–89	Paul R. West
1989–90	Norma I. Mickelson
1990–93	Bruce E. More
1993–95	William W. Wadge
1995–97	Rodney T.K. Symington
1998–2000	Tom Cleary
2000–02	William E. Pfaffenberger
2002–04	James A. Dopp
2004–05	Andrew Weaver
2005–07	William E. Pfaffenberger
2007–08	Mary Sanseverino
2008–present	Leslie Francis Pelton

APPENDIX 6: PRESIDENTS/CHAIRPERSONS, UNIVERSITY OF VICTORIA ALMA MATER SOCIETY AND UNIVERSITY OF VICTORIA STUDENTS' SOCIETY

Presidents/Chairpersons, University of Victoria Alma Mater Society

1962–63	Alfred J.L Pettersen
1963–64	Laurence E. Devlin
1964–65	Olivia R. Barr
1965–66	L. Paul Williamson
1966–67	Stephen A. Bigsby
1967–68	David L. McLean

1968–69	Frank D. Frketich
1969–70	Norman T. Wright
1970–71	Robert P. McDougall
1971–72	Ian J. McKinnon
1972–73	Russell W.E. Freethy
1973 (June–October)	David C. Clode
1973–74	Linda M. Flavelle
1974–75	Kirk R. Patterson
1975–76	Clayton J. Shold
1976–77	J. Alistair Palmer
1977–78	Brian L. Gardiner
1978–79	David D. Connell
1979–80	Marla R. Nickerson
1980–81	Angus A.S. Christian
1981–82	P. Timothy Winkelmans
1982–83	Eric L. Hargreaves
1983–84	Brian J. Stevenson
1984–85	Joanne M. Howard & Rosemin Keshvani
1985–86	Rosemin Keshvani
1986–87	Monica Maier & Klaus J. Mulert
1987–88	Pamela R. Frache
1988–89	Susanne M. Klausen

Presidents, University of Victoria Students' Society

1989–90	Lise-Lotte E. Loomer
1990–91	Howard Jampolsky

Chairpersons, University of Victoria Students' Society

1991–92	Oona T. Padgham
1992–93	Dayna L. Christ
1993–94	Janetta S. Ozard
1994–95	Tina Walker
1995–96	Tina Walker
1996–97	Ian Flemington
1997–98	Theresa Sabourin
1998–99	Rob Fleming
1999–2000	Morgan Stewart
2001–02	Jamie Matten

2002–03	Troy Sebastien
2003–04	Jude Groves
2004–05	Joanna Groves
2005–06	Penny Beames
2006–07	Penny Beames
2007–08	Tracy Ho
2008–09	Caitlin Meggs
2009–10	Veronica Harrison
2010–11	James Coccola
2011–12	Tara Paterson

....

APPENDIX 7: PRESIDENTS OF THE GRADUATE STUDENTS' SOCIETY

The Graduate Students' Society existed informally until 1984, when it was incorporated.

1966–67	Padraig A. Coughlan
1967–68	Michael G. Roberts
1968–69	Fred F. Hyslop
1970–71	Murray J. King
1971–72	John N. Dorner
1972–73	Eric S. Lee
1973–74	James B. London
1974–75	Anne D. Forester
1975–76	Richard J. Thomas
1976–77	Albert L. Rydant & Stephen B. McClellan
1977–79	Mark A. Hallam
1979–80	Thomas J. Crabtree
1980–81	James A. Soles
1981–82	Andrew Shand
1982–83	Edwin J. Zemek
1983–84	Neville N. Winchester
1984–85	Christopher J. Morry
1985–86	Peter W. Demeo
1986–87	Kash Dehgan
1987–88	Thomas J. Perry
1988–89	Benjamin Dorman

1989–91	Douglas L. Tolson
1991–92	John F. Dower
1992–94	Carrie L. Bronson
1994–95	Jeremy Mannall-Fretwell
1995–96	Kathryn Sutherland
1996–98	Mike Conlan
1998–2000	Sandra Guarascio
2000–01	Olga Rinco
2001–02	Olga Rinco/Gabe Haythornthwaite
2002–03	Gabe Haythornthwaite/Basil Alexander
2003–04	Basil Alexander
2004–05	Chris Hurl
2005–06	Tayfun Ince
2006–07	Amanda Finn
2007–08	Patrick Reed
2008–09	Nicole O'Byrne
2009–10	Adrienne Canning
2010–11	Kalin McClusky/Adrienne Canning
2011–present	Julia Munk

APPENDIX 8: PRESIDENTS OF UNIVERSITY OF VICTORIA UNIONS

CUPE 917 (outside workers, food services, maintenance, janitorial)

1986–91	Ron Cullen
1991–93	Art Reynolds
1993–95	Ron Cullen
1995–97	Bernie Guenster
1997–2002	Rhonda Rose
2002–present	Rob Park

CUPE 951 (office, technical, and childcare workers)

1971–81	Edna Kowalchuk
1981–84	Liliane Morgan
1985–87	Geraldine McGuire
1988–92	Bill Johnstone
1993–present	Doug Sprenger

CUPE 4163 (University of Victoria Educational Employees' Union)

1998	Shawn Bishop
1998–99	Melissa Svensen
1999–2000	Charlotte Sheldrake
2000–02	Ted Allison
2002–03	Ian Cameron
2003–04	Marianna Vetricci
2004–05	Ian Cameron
2005–06	David Millar
2006–07	Peter Hampton
2007–08	Dave McKercher
2008–09	Victor Lorentz/Dave McKercher
2009–10	Craig Ashbourne
2010–11	Craig Ashbourne/Josephine MacIntosh
2011–present	Drew Farrance

NOTES

All interviews cited in these endnotes were undertaken by the author in Victoria. Copies of them will be placed in the UVic Archives in late 2012.

CHAPTER ONE

1 Peter Smith, *A Multitude of the Wise: UVic Remembered* (Victoria: The Alumni Association of the University of Victoria, 1993), 26.

CHAPTER TWO

1 Terry Rekston, *Rattenbury* (Victoria: Sono Nis Press, 1978), 95–6.
2 Smith, *A Multitude of the Wise*, 42.

CHAPTER THREE

1 Smith, *A Multitude of the Wise*, 60.
2 Pierre Berton, *Starting Out, 1920–1947* (Toronto: McClelland and Stewart, 1987), 119–23.
3 Pierre Berton studied at Victoria College for two academic years, 1937–38 and 1938–39. He found his studies to be largely a continuation of high school and was later critical of that, but he also found the writing career that made him famous in Canada. To some extent, that was because of an English teacher, Miss Jeanette Cann. Berton's biographer, A.B. McKillop, recently wrote: "His first essay for her was on the departure of the last steamboat heading upriver from Dawson before freeze-up in the fall, chock full with the kind of detail that paints pictures in the reader's mind … She rewarded his efforts with an A+ and praised him in front of the class. 'From that moment on,' Berton later said, 'she encouraged me constantly to write and, basking in the warmth of that approval, I wrote.' Miss Cann's standards were high. In spite of her interest in Pierre's work, his final grade in English – 73 per cent – was a little lower than that of the year before." A.B. McKillop, *Pierre Berton, A Biography* (Toronto: McClelland & Stewart, 2010), 92–3.
4 Interview, Reg Roy, 26 August 2010.
5 Ian Tyson, *The Long Trail: My Life in the West* (Toronto: Random House, 2010), 31.
6 Edward B. Harvey, *The Lansdowne Era: Victoria College, 1946–1963* (Montreal and Kingston: McGill-Queen's University Press, 2008).
7 Smith, *A Multitude of the Wise*, 122.

CHAPTER FOUR

1 Communication to the author from Martin Segger, 1 November 2011.

CHAPTER FIVE

1 Interview, Chris Petter, 4 May 2010.
2 Smith, *A Multitude of the Wise*, 148–9.
3 Ibid., 138.
4 Interview, Chris Petter, 4 May 2010.
5 Smith, *A Multitude of the Wise*, 138.
6 University of Victoria, *Report of the President, 1964–65* (Victoria: University of Victoria, 1966), 11 (available in UVic Archives).
7 Interview, Trevor Matthews, 9 February 2010.
8 See http://www.triumf.ca/about-triumf/about-us/history.
9 Smith, *A Multitude of the Wise*, 164.
10 Ibid., 172–3.
11 Interview, Jenny Waelti-Walters, French Department, Women's Studies Department, 4 August 2010.

CHAPTER SIX

1 Interview, Howard Petch, 26 April 2010.
2 University of Victoria, *Report of the President 1973–74* (Victoria: University of Victoria, undated), 20.
3 For example, Currie established that only 40 per cent of the engineers hired in BC at the time came from UBC; the rest came from outside the province. (Interview, H.E. Petch, 26 April 2010).
4 Interview, Howard Petch, 26 April 2010.
5 Ibid., 26 April 2010 and 5 May 2010.
6 Margaret R. Scaia and Lynne E. Young, "Writing History: Case Study of the University of Victoria School of Nursing" (unpublished paper, 2009), 3.
7 Interview, David Glen, 24 August 2010.
8 Interview, William Neilson, 29 April 2010.
9 Interview, Anne Fraser, 21 January 2011.
10 Interview, Len Bruton, 12 August 2010.
11 The perspectives of the engaged faculty members ultimately appeared in a rather controversial book that was widely discussed: Warren Magnusson, *The New Reality: The Politics of Restraint in British Columbia* (Vancouver: New Star Books, 1985).
12 Interview, Eric Manning, 10 May 2010.

13 *UVic Fulltime Faculty Head Count by Gender (All Ranks)*, Historical data provided by the Department of Institutional Planning and Analysis, University of Victoria, May 2011. For current data see www.inst.uvic.ca/faculty.html.
14 Victoria Women's Movement Archives, Special Collections, University of Victoria Women's Centre Fonds, AR 225.
15 Interview, Jennifer Waelti-Walters, 4 August 2010.
16 Ibid.
17 Ibid.
18 Rachel Carson, *Silent Spring* (Boston: Houghton Mifflin, 1962; Boston: Mariner Books, 2002). Several copies of this book are still stocked in the UVic bookstore.
19 Alan Drengson, "Environmental Studies from the Early Years: Impressionistic Reflections" (paper written for School of Environmental Studies, University of Victoria, July 2010), 1, http://web.uvic.ca/enweb/history.php.
20 Ibid., 6.
21 Ibid.
22 Interview, John Tucker, 14 April 2011.
23 See "Kingdom of Antir," http://www.antir.sca.org/Map/.
24 Interview, Alex McAuley, 17 December 2010.
25 Interview, Sam Scully, 15 August 2010.
26 *University of Victoria Undergraduate and Graduate Headcounts, 1963/64 – 2010/11* and *Historical Faculty Headcounts by Gender (All Ranks)*, Department of Institutional Planning and Analysis, University of Victoria, May 2011. For last three years' statistics see http://www.inst.uvic.ca/faculty.html.
27 University of Victoria, *Five Year Review, 1985–1990* (Office of the President, 1991), 7.
28 Interview, Howard Petch, 5 May 2011.
29 Ibid.
30 Interview, David Glen, 24 August 2010.
31 Interview, Ken Shields, 28 September 2010.
32 Interview, Larry Devlin, 7 January 2011.
33 Ibid.
34 See Ron Faris, *The Passionate Educators: Voluntary Associations and The Struggle for Control of Adult*

Educational Broadcasting in Canada, 1919–52 (Toronto: P. Martin Associates, 1975).
35 Interview, Len Bruton, 12 August 2010.
36 See "An Honourable Alum," *The Torch: The University of Victoria Alumni Magazine*, Autumn (2000), 4, http://web.uvic.ca/torch/.

CHAPTER SEVEN

1 Memorial University College opened in 1925 as a college of Oxford University; it became Memorial University in 1949.
2 See *The Ring* (UVic campus paper), "Installation Fest draws 30,000 spectators," 23 November 1990, 3, special insert, 15 October 1990, and coverage in the issue of 13 November 1990, 3.
3 The author is indebted to Helen Kempster, who for many years was in charge of ceremonies and special events at UVic, for her recollections of this event.
4 Interview, David Strong, 11 February 2011.
5 Ibid.
6 The impact of internationalization on academic institutions can be profound, with negative as well as positive effects. It also raises questions about relationships to globalization (the integration of economic forces and institutions) and how they can and should be considered and "managed" within universities. For a stimulating discussion of some of the issues involved, see Felix Maringe and Nick Fossett, *Globalization and Internationalization in Higher Education: Theoretical, Strategic and Management Perspectives* (London: Continuum International Publishing Group, 2010).
7 *UVic Report, 1998* (Victoria: University of Victoria, Office of the President, 1999), 12.
8 Interview, William Neilson, 29 April 2010.
9 *UVic Report, 1998*, 6.
10 For fuller discussions of the ways in which "massification" affected universities, see Harold C. Clark, *Growth and Governance of Canadian Universities* (Vancouver: UBC Press, 2004) and James A. Côté and Anton L. Allahar, *Lowering Higher Education: The Rise of Corporate Universities and the Fall of*

Liberal Education (Toronto: University of Toronto Press, 2011).

11 See several short articles, *The Ring*, 4 September 1992, 6–7.

12 *UVic Report, 1998*, 16.

13 Patty Pitts, "International Movement Comes to UVic to Explore Students' First Year Experience," *The Ring*, 24 April 1992, 3.

14 "Chancellor Questions 'Antediluvian Lecture System,'" *The Ring*, 10 December 1990, 2.

15 "Grad Studies to Celebrate Anniversary in March," *The Ring*, 9 December 1991, 3.

16 Memo to the author, Stacy Chappel, "University of Victoria Graduate Students' Society: A Brief History," 10 July 2011. A copy of this memo will be placed in the UVic Archives along with other papers used in the preparation of this book.

17 David Clode served as the manager of the Alma Mater Society from 1975 to 1989, assistant director of Student and Ancillary Services from 1989 to 1998, and as director of Student and Ancillary Services from 1998 until 2009. Interview, David Clode, 9 June 2010.

18 Ibid.

19 "Co-operative Education: Expanding with Care," *The Ring*, 10 December 1990, 4.

20 The Interfaith Chaplaincy began in 1974 with a Roman Catholic priest, Father Leo Robert; an Anglican priest, Marlowe Anderson; and a United Church minister, Clare Homes.

21 From an introductory Canadian history class taught by the author in the early 1990s.

22 Interview, Sam Scully, 10 August 2010.

23 Ibid.

24 Donna Danylchuk, "Health Promotion Will be Direction of Future University Health Care Education," *The Ring*, 30 September 1991, 4–5.

25 For a synopsis of the report, see "Summary Report on Harassment Policy and Procedures Review," *The Ring*, 26 November 1993, 3. See also "Advisor Reports on Concerns of Women Faculty," *The Ring*, 10 December 1993.

26 "Equity Policy for Female Faculty Members, Approved by the UVic Board of Governors, April 17, 1990," *The Ring*, 10 December 1990, 7.

27 Interview, David Strong, 11 February 2011.

28 Teresa Moore, "UVic's Innovation Development Corporation – Five Years of Success," *The Ring*, 9 May 1997, 2.

29 "Speakers Bureau reaches 10,000," *The Ring*, 11 April 1997, http://ring.uvic.ca/97apr11/speakers_bureau.html.

CHAPTER EIGHT

1 Interview, David Turpin, 28 February 2011.

2 "Board Approves Student Housing Expansion," *The Ring*, 29 November 2001.

3 Mathematics and Statistics Assistance Centre, University of Victoria, www.math.uvic.ca. The centre is one of the programmes offered by the Learning and Teaching Centre.

4 See *The Revitalization of Undergraduate Education in Canada: A Report on the AUCC Workshop on Undergraduate Education in Halifax, March 6–8, 2011*, available on the AUCC website: http://www.aucc.ca/policy-issues/undergraduate-education/.

5 Pierre Zundel and Patrick Deane, "It's Time to Transform Undergraduate Education," *University Affairs*, 6 December 2010, http://www.universityaffairs.ca/its-time-to-transform-undergraduate-education.aspx.

6 The increases have taken place. In 2003, there were just over 3,000 student awards distributing just over $4 million; in 2009–10, there were over 5,000 awards distributing $8 million annually. Historical record provided by Institutional Analysis, University of Victoria. Most recent statistics tabulated from website of the Office of the Registrar, University of Victoria, http://registrar.uvic.ca/safa/scholarships/scholarshipmedalprize.html.

7 Alicia Ulysses, personal communication to the author, 13 September 2011.

8 Statistics provided by the Faculty of Graduate Studies.

9 Maria Lironi, "Survey Examines Barriers to Degree Completion," *The Ring*, March 2004, 3.

10 Interview, Jamie Cassels, 9 December 2010.

11 Ibid.

12 Interview, Doug Sprenger, 20 July 2010.

13 Canada Foundation for Innovation and Re$earch Infosource (2007–08 FT Faculty). See http://www.researchinfosource.com/. Re$earch Infosource is a division of The Impact Group and, among its activities, independently monitors spending on research within universities and the private sector in Canada.

14 Valerie Shore, "$62 Million Partnership Will Revolutionize Ocean Science," *The Ring*, 6 November 2003, http://ring.uvic.ca/03nov06/news/index.html.

15 In 2007, UVic established Ocean Networks Canada to oversee NEPTUNE Canada and VENUS. In 2009, the Ocean Networks Canada Centre for Enterprise and Engagement, a national centre of excellence for commercialisation and outreach, was added to facilitate economic development and to ensure that the new knowledge being gained was made readily available to policy makers and others. The work of ONC, now headed by Martin Taylor, has major implications for a wide range of economic, research, and technological issues. See http://www.oceannetworks.ca/.

16 Gregory Mone, Brooke Borel, Katherine Bagley, and Jennifer Abbasi, "Big Science: The Universe's Ten Most Epic Projects," *Popular Science*, 16 July 2011, http://www.popsci.com/science/gallery/2011-07/big-science-universes-ten-most-epic-projects.

17 "Seven UVic-based Scientists Sit on UN Climate Panel," *The Ring*, 8 July 2004, http://ring.uvic.ca/04july08/news/climate.html.

18 See The Honorable Iona Campagnolo, Lieutenant Governor, *Speech from the Throne* (at the opening of the third Session, thirty-eighth parliament of the province of British Columbia), 13 February 2007, http://www.leg.bc.ca/38th3rd/4-8-38-3.htm.

19 Interview, David Turpin, 28 February 2011.

20 See Pacific Institute for Climate Solutions, "Research," http://www.pics.uvic.ca/research.php.

21 See Jeffrey Foss, *Beyond Environmentalism: Towards a Philosophy of Nature* (Hoboken, NJ: John Wiley & Sons, 2009).

22 Memo from Michel Lefebvre, 28 September 2011.

23 Ibid.
24 Ibid.
25 For example, see Rennie Warburton, "Beyond the Mainstream," *The Ring*, 5 September 2002, and the report, *Voices for Change*, which Warburton co-authored with Yvonne Martin-Newcombe (Communication and Social Foundations) in 1998. The report examines UVic's record with regard to racial, ethnic, and cultural minorities. See http://ring.uvic.ca/98may08/Voices.html.
26 See Jochen R. Moehr, Denis J. Protti, Francis Y. Lau, and Nicole A. Grimm, "Project Based Experiential Distance Education: An Oxymoron," *International Journal of Medical Informatics* 73, no. 2 (18 March 2004): 157–63.
27 "UVic Shines in 2010 National Research Rankings," University of Victoria media release, 21 October 2010, http://communications.uvic.ca/releases/release.php?display=release&id=1173.

CHAPTER NINE

1 Statistics from *The Revitalization of Undergraduate Education in Canada, A report on the AUCC Workshop on Undergraduate Education in Halifax, March 6–8, 2011* (Ottawa: AUCC, 2011), 1; and from AUCC website http://www.aucc.ca/canadian-universities/facts-and-stats/.
2 Interview, David Turpin, 28 February 2011.

INDEX